COOL JAPAN

SUMIKO KAJIYAMA

Museyon, New York

Library of Congress Cataloging-in-Publication Data

Names: Kajiyama, Sumiko, 1963- author.
Title: Cool Japan : a guide to Tokyo, Kyoto, Tohoku and Japanese culture past and present / Sumiko Kajiyama.
Description: 2nd edition. | New York : Museyon, 2018. | Series: Cool Japan series ; Book 1
Identifiers: LCCN 2017059883 (print) | LCCN 2017060689 (ebook) | ISBN 9781938450976 | ISBN 9781938450983 | ISBN 9781938450990 | ISBN 9781940842226 (paperback)
Subjects: LCSH: Tokyo (Japan)--Guidebooks. | Kyoto (Japan)--Guidebooks. | Tōhoku Region (Japan)--Guidebooks. | Japan--Civilization--21st century. | BISAC: TRAVEL / Asia / Japan. | HISTORY / Asia / Japan.
Classification: LCC DS896.38 (ebook) | LCC DS896.38 .K35 2018 (print) | DDC 952.05--dc23
LC record available at https://lccn.loc.gov/2017059883

Published in the United States by:
Museyon Inc.
333 East 45th Street
New York, NY 10017

Museyon is a registered trademark.
Visit us online at www.museyon.com

ISBN 978-1-940842-22-6

815110

Printed in China

May they not forget to keep pure the great heritage that puts them ahead of the West: the artistic configuration of life, the simplicity and modesty of personal needs, and the purity and serenity of the Japanese soul.

—Albert Einstein, 1922

京都 KYOTO 10

東京 TOKYO 122

CONTENTS

東北 TOHOKU *198*

Hometown of Heart for Japanese People

All names are shown in the Japanese style: Family name first, given
name second

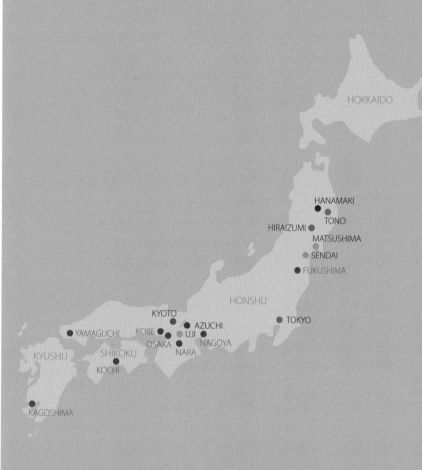

THE FOUR MAIN ISLANDS OF JAPAN

HOKKAIDO

HANAMAKI
TONO
HIRAIZUMI
MATSUSHIMA
SENDAI
FUKUSHIMA

HONSHU

KYOTO
AZUCHI
YAMAGUCHI
KOBE
UJI
TOKYO
OSAKA
NAGOYA
NARA
KYUSHU
SHIKOKU
KOCHI

KAGOSHIMA

THE HISTORY OF JAPAN (14000 BC - 1931)

JOMON / YAYOI 14,000BC - 300	Earliest Japanese settlers are hunters, gatherers and fishermen Origins of rice agriculture
KOFUN 300 – 592	Powerful leaders arise and build large tombs (*kofun*) Around 350: Japan is united by the Yamato court for the first time 538: Introduction of Buddhism from China
ASUKA 592 – 710	645: The era of the Fujiwara family begins after the Taika Reform
NARA 710 – 784	710: Nara becomes the first permanent capital 784: The capital is moved to Nagaoka
HEIAN 794 – 1185	794: The capital is moved to Heian (Kyoto) 1010: Murasaki Shkibu releases *The Tale of Genji* 1159: Taira clan takes power after the Heiji War 1180 - 85: Minamoto clan puts an end to Taira supremacy in the Genpei War 1187: Minamoto Yoshitsune flees to Hiraizumi for Fujiwara protection
KAMAKURA 1192 – 1333	1192: Minamoto Yoritomo appointed shogun by the emperor and establishes the Kamakura shogunate 1274, 1281: Mongol invasion attemts are thwarted by stormy weather
MUROMACHI 1338 – 1573	1338: Ashikaga Takauji establishes the Muromachi shogunate in Kyoto 1467 – 1477: Onin War destroys Kyoto 1542: Firearms and Christianity are introduced to Japan by the Portuguese 1568: Oda Nobunaga enters Kyoto
AZUCHI / **MOMOYAMA** 1573 – 1603	1575: Takeda clan is defeated by Nobunaga at the battle of Nagashino 1582: Nobunaga is killed at Honno-ji and succeeded by Toyotomi Hideyoshi 1590: Japan is reunited by Hideyoshi 1600: Tokugawa Ieyasu wins the Battle of Sekigahara after Hideyoshi's death
EDO 1603 – 1868	1603: Ieyasu is appointed shogun and establishes his shogunate in Edo (Tokyo) 1639: *Sakoku* (isolation) policy is adopted; Japan closes its doors to the world 1689: Matsuo Basho leaves Edo for his journey to Tohoku 1854: Commodore Perry of United States forces Japan to open ports for trade 1867: Sakamoto Ryoma is murdered at the Omiya inn in Kyoto in 1867
MEIJI 1868 – 1912	1868: Emperor Meiji ushers in the Meiji Restoration and moves the capital to Tokyo
TAISHO / SHOWA 1912 – 1989	1931: Miyazawa Kenji writes a poem, "Unbeaten by Rain," in his small journal

COOL JAPAN

KYOTO

京都

Geiko And Maiko Celebrate New Year in Kyoto

Kyoto and The Three Beloved Heroes

Kyoto's Three Heroes: Murasaki Shikibu, Oda Nobunaga, and Sakamoto Ryoma

History and modern culture coexist in Japan.

The old capital city, Kyoto, is a prime example. Emperor Kammu decided to make this city his capital in 794. Even now, you can find remnants of those days when you walk around the city. The city's layout in a grid-like pattern is itself the very image of Heian-kyo (which means tranquility and peace capital), Kyoto's old name.

The city has never stopped evolving in its 1,200-year history. Despite construction restrictions on building heights meant to preserve the city's famous vistas, there are modern buildings. Likewise, people walk about the streets dressed in contemporary fashions while sipping on Starbucks lattés— just as you would see in Ginza or Harajuku in Tokyo.

Modern Gion Matsuri celebrations; *Gion Matsuri in Rakutyu Rakugai-zu,* by Kano Eitoku, 1540-1560s, Uesugi Museum

Kyoto was the national capital for over 1,000 years, from 794 until 1868, and its landmarks have a wide range of historic backgrounds. One of the most popular places to visit in Kyoto, the dazzling Kinkaku-ji (The Golden Pavilion), was built at the end of the 14th century, during the Muromachi period, while the famous geisha district, Gion, was most prosperous in the beginning of the 19th century, the latter part of the Edo period.

People jokingly say that if an elderly Kyoto resident mentions "the last war", he or she means the Onin War of the 15th century, not World War II. The center of Kyoto was burned down during the Onin War, while it was left untouched by WWII.

Fall foliage over Kiyomizu-dera with a view of Kyoto City

Because the city was spared during WWII, many of the cultural properties and faces of historic centers were saved and maintained to this day. It may be surprising to some people that a culture built with flammable wood and paper has been kept intact for such a long period of time.

You can find the footsteps of people who lived in a various periods in the past in this not-so-big city. In this way, you can easily travel through time as you travel through Kyoto.

Through the tales of three of Japan's most famous heroes—Hikaru Genji (and his creator, Murasaki Shikibu), Oda Nobunaga and Sakamoto Ryoma—you can experience over 1,000 years in this uniquely historic city.

History lives on in modern Kyoto. Clockwise, from top left: Philosophers Walk; Maiko; Nanzen-ji; Ryoan-ji temple; Togetsukyo Bridge in Arashiyama; Sanzen-in

KYOTO

LADY MURASAKI & THE TALE OF GENJI

1. KYOTO IMPERIAL PALACE
2. HEIAN JINGU SHRINE
3. KAMIGAMO SHRINE
4. SHIMOGAMO SHRINE
5. DAIKAKU-JI TEMPLE
6. SHOSEI-EN GARDEN
7. ROSAN-JI TEMPLE—
   LADY MURASAKI'S RESIDENCE
8. URIN-IN TEMPLE
9. HEIAN COSTUME EXPERIENCE STUDIO

ODA NOBUNAGA

1. SHOKOKU-JI TEMPLE
2. JOTENKAKU MUSEUM
3. KINKAKU-JI TEMPLE
4. GINKAKU-JI TEMPLE
5. MYOKAKU-JI TEMPLE
6. DAITOKU-JI TEMPLE SOKEN-IN
7. NIJO CASTLE

SAKAMOTO RYOMA

1. TERADAYA INN
2. JIKKOKU-BUNE BOAT
3. GEKKEIKAN OKURA SAKE MUSEUM
4. KIZAKURA KINENNKAN
5. MARUYAMA PARK
6. KYOTO RYOSEN GOKOKU SHRINE AND
   THE RYOSEN HISTORY MUSEUM
7. AKEBONO-TEI
8. SUYA
9. SUMI-YA MOTENASHI ART MUSEUM
10. WACHIGAI-YA

🏯 Temple   ⛩ Shrine

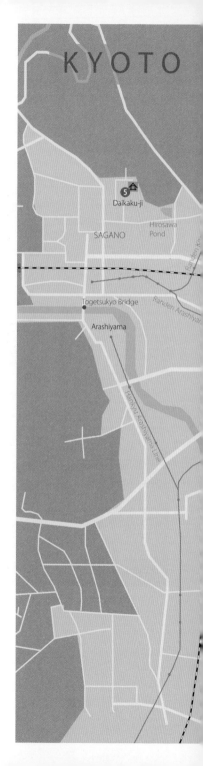

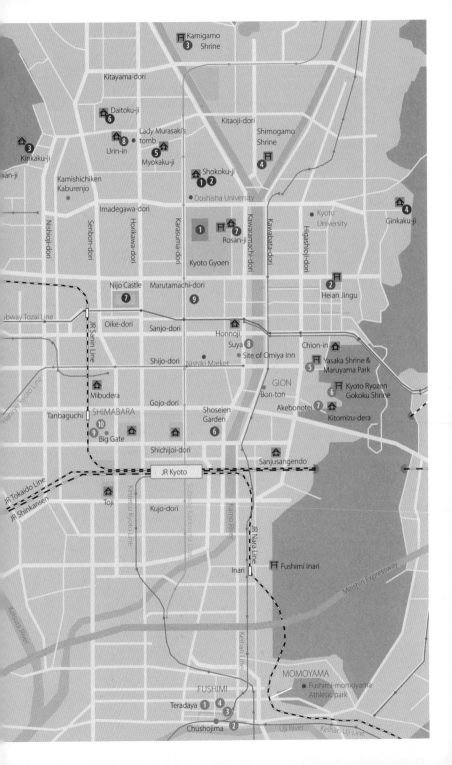

紫式部
MURASAKI SHIKIBU

The *Genji Monogatari Emaki, Kashiwagi* (detail), Heian Period, Tokugawa Art Museum

Murasaki Shikibu, the Court Lady Who Wrote the First Modern Novel

The Tale of Genji vividly portrays the lifestyle inside the palace of the Heian capital 1,000 years ago, a time when the powerful Fujiwara clan dominated Japan. Widely regarded as the world's first modern novel, *The Tale of Genji* was written by Murasaki Shikibu, a woman of the court, in the middle of the Heian period. The majestic novel has attracted readers for over 1,000 years in various translations in modern Japanese, as well as in many foreign languages.

Let the hero of this novel, Hikaru Genji, be your guide to Kyoto's Heian-era sites.

Although Genji is a fictional character, his image exists clearly among the Japanese. "Who was the biggest ladies' man in Japanese history?" Many Japanese would name Hikaru Genji. He was a prince of the emperor, blessed with brilliant beauty and unparalleled talent. He was a superstar who was unbeatable both in sword and pen, in music, dance, and romance. He was surely popular and his love affairs were the talk of the town.

The Shishinden, or main hall, at Kyoto Gosho

"Hikaru Kimi" (the shining prince) is still the timeless dream boy for the ladies.

However, this novel is not just pulp entertainment like a Harlequin romance. Its underlying theme is the Buddhist concept of the impermanence of worldly things. Human ego, jealousy, greed for power, cunning, and purity—*The Tale of Genji* depicts such immutable aspects of human nature. This story has been made into movies, manga, and animated films, and still resonates with people in the 21st century.

Kyoto Gosho

The Tale of Genji is a work of fiction but many shrines and temples that were the models or backdrops of the story remain in Kyoto.

The most famous of all is Kyoto Gosho (the Imperial Palace) where the emperor's family resided and royal ceremonies and rituals took place. The successive emperors actually lived here until Emperor Meiji relocated the capital to Tokyo in 1869 after returning to power when the Meiji Restoration ended shogun warrior rule.

LADY MURASAKI & THE TALE OF GENJI

Being a prince of the emperor, Hikaru Genji would have been born in this palace.

Strictly speaking, however, the current palace was rebuilt in 1855 in the end of the Edo period. Even though it is built in Heian style, its location is different from the original palace.

The original Heian palace burned down in the 13th century and was never rebuilt. The current palace was the emperor's regent's mansion where the emperor stayed temporarily, and which was enlarged with the help of warlords in the Warring States Period (Sengoku Jidai). The building itself was burned down and rebuilt again many times until the current structure was built 150 years ago.

The central area of the Heian capital was a rectangle of about 0.72 miles (1.2 km) from east to west and 0.84 miles (1.4 km) from north to south. The emperor's residence and administrative buildings were all located within this area.

The grid-like layout of the city remains as it was originally. However, the main boulevard in the central area, Suzaku Oji, used to be as wide as 275 feet (84 meters). Senbon-dori Street now runs north to south where the Suzaku Oji was once laid out, but

WHAT IS THE TALE OF GENJI?

Widely accepted as the world's first novel, *The Tale of Genji* depicts romance and the life of the nobility in the court of the Heian period. Written by Murasaki Shikibu, the story portrays three generations surrounding the main character, Hikaru Genji, as he encounters various types of women and matures as a man and as a person.

As many as 500 characters appear in this tightly structured story, which features vivid everyday conversations and scenes of court culture, as well as Japan's rich seasons. While it is a charming romance novel of fragile love affairs, Buddhist philosophy about the transience of human life is the undercurrent of the story.

Love, hate, and suffering in the lives of the women who have relationships with Genji bring out deep sympathy from the reader regardless of distance in time and culture. Some readers claim that they find the full portrayal of human nature and man's reality through Hikaru Genji.

In 2008, the Kyoto government carried out a special event, The Millennium of The Tale of Genji, to commemorate this extraordinary literature that has entertained many readers around the world for the past 1,000 years.

HEIAN CAPITAL & KYOTO GOSHO

THE IMPERIAL PALACE

Kyoto Imperial Palace, or Kyoto Gosho, was the Imperial Palace of Japan and housed the Imperial Family from the Heian period until the capital was moved to Tokyo in 1868 during the Meiji Restoration. Located in Kyoto Gyoen Park, the palace, as it is today, was rebuilt in 1855 in the Heian architecture style, following a fire. It was the eighth time the palace was rebuilt since it was first built in 794.

The palace grounds include a number of buildings, including the Imperial Residence, the residence of the retired emperor, and even a university. The main building boasts a number of historically important halls, including the Shishinden (the ceremonial hall where emperors were crowned), the Seiryoden (once the Emperor's private residence), the Kogosho (small palace), the Ogakumonjo, and the Otsunegoten.

The grounds are open to the public (none of the buildings can be entered), but appointments must be made with the Imperial Household Agency, which also provides guided tours.

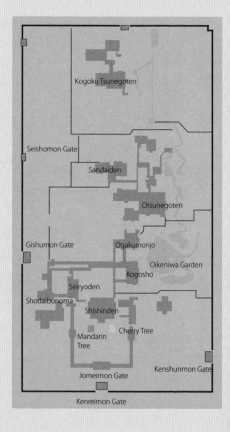

LADY MURASAKI & THE TALE OF GENJI

A scene at the Seiryoden from the *Genji Monogatari Emaki,* Tokugawa Art Museum

it is only 82 feet (25 meters) at its the widest and merely 20 feet (6 meters) wide where it is the narrowest.

A 275-foot-wide (84-meter) street is more like a plaza than a street. Noblemen and noblewomen riding on their oxcarts would pass each other on this street 1,000 years ago.

Even though the current Kyoto Gosho palace is not the same building where *The Tale of Genji* took place, its atmosphere recalls those days.

Kyoto Gosho has six gates and each of them is designated for different ranks and usages. Though the emperor no longer lives here, the palace is still managed by the Imperial Household Agency. Reservations must be made before visiting. However, in spring and fall, it opens its doors to public and attracts many tourists.

Once you cross the gate, you will feel the air turn solemn in the palace. The must-see spots are the Seiryoden, where the emperor would perform his daily duties, and the Shishinden, where the most important rituals, including the accession ceremonies, would take place.

Seiryoden

Inside the magnificent Shishinden, with its arching cypress bark roof, sits the emperor's throne, Takamikura (Chrysanthemum Throne), facing the white-stone courtyard, Dantei. In *The Tale of Genji*, Hikaru Genji had his coming-of-age ceremony here. He was so loved by his father, the Emperor Kiritsubo, after his mother passed away that his ceremony was specially held in this highest-rank room.

You can imagine how beautiful it would be as Hikaru Genji, dressed up in a colorful costume, danced elegantly in this room. The ladies in the palace would stare through the bamboo blinds and sigh for the shining prince.

In the Dantei courtyard, there are two glorious trees: the "Sakon-no-Sakura" cherry blossom tree on the left side and "Ukon-no-Tachibana" mandarin orange tree on the right side, as viewed from the Shishinden. Many shrines in Japan have such paired cherry and mandarin orange trees, but this pair is exceptional in size and grandeur.

LADY MURASAKI & THE TALE OF GENJI

A kemari demonstration at Kyoto Gosho

HIKARU GENJI

Hikaru Genji's mother, Kiritsubo-no-koi, was the emperor's favorite wife among many that he had. However, because her father's rank was lower than those of other wives' fathers, she had the lower title for a wife of the emperor, Koi. The higher-rank court ladies catering to the emperor in his sleeping quarters were jealous of Kiritsubo-no-koi and often picked on her.

With a low-ranking mother, Genji's path to the throne was difficult in spite of his charm and talent. Adding to his struggle, his maternal grandfather passed away early and his mother died when he was three. He lacked crucial political backing, and had insecure status. Emperor Kiritsubo, Genji's father, made the difficult decision to demote the boy to vassal out of his true affection. After that, Genji made his way up with the emperor's confidence and captured the hearts of many court ladies with his beauty.

GENJI

Genji is an alternate name for members of the Minamoto family, people demoted from the imperial family into the nobility. Some of them turned into samurai. The most famous Genji in Japanese history is the founder of the 12th-century Kamakura Government, shogun Minamoto Yoritomo, or perhaps his younger brother, the warrior Minamoto Yoshitsune.

In Japan, people still celebrate the growth of their children every March on Hina Matsuri (Girls' Day) by displaying Heian-style dolls. They have miniature paired "Sakon-no-Sakura" and "Ukon-no-Tachibana" trees to complete the set.

Today, Kyoto Gosho is located within the extensive park called Kyoto Gyoen. More than 200 mansions of noble families once stood here. They all moved out when the Emperor moved to Tokyo after the Meiji Restoration in 1869.

Kyoto Gyoen is open to public and it is a green oasis in the city. There are some ruins of old mansions and gardens of the Heian court nobles that you can visit. There are 1,100 cherry trees in the park and the blossoms are spectacular in spring. A famous *ito zakura*

Hikaru Genji accepts the illegitimate son, Kaoru. Kashiwagi scene from *Genji Monigatari Emaki*, 12th century, Tokugawa Art Museum

THE TALE OF GENJI SYNOPSIS

There was a prince whose father was Emperor Kiritsubo and mother was one of the Kois, the lower-rank court ladies who worked in the emperor's sleeping quarters. The emperor cherished this Koi regardless of her rank and their son grew up so beautiful and smart that people called him "shining prince." But the boy's mother passed away while he was still very young. Worried about the future of this young son, the emperor gave him the surname Minamoto (or Gen-ji) and demoted him to vassal status. He is the hero of the novel, Hikaru Genji.

The emperor's new wife, Fujitsubo, looked like the late Koi, and he cherished her very much. Hikaru Genji also fell in love with her, looking for the image of his late mother. He finally pursued his forbidden love and Fujitsubo gave birth to his boy, who was raised as the tenth prince of Emperor Kiritsubo and later became the emperor himself.

Hikaru Genji married Aoi-no-ue, a daughter of another powerful family. The couple was blessed with a boy Yugiri, but their relationship was distant. The cadish Genji had affairs with many ladies, including Yugao, whom he romanced without even knowing her name; Suetsumu-hana, a daughter of a fallen royal; Rokujyo-no-miyasudokoro, a widow of the late prince; Oborozukiyo, a daughter of an elite family; and others.

After losing his wife Aoi-no-ue, Genji married Fujitsubo's niece and lookalike, Murasaki-no-ue. He had adopted her when she was very young and had been raising her to be his ideal woman. Later, when he was exiled to Suma, he met Akashi-no-kimi and had a baby girl between them, who would later become empress.

Genji kept rising in rank and had a mansion called Rokujyo-in where his wives lived together. While he was

LADY MURASAKI & THE TALE OF GENJI

enjoying his prosperity, former Emperor Suzaku-in forced him marry his niece, Onna-sannomiya. Murasaki-no-ue agonized over his new wife and this troubled Genji. As time passed, his best friend's son, Kashiwagi, committed adultery with Onna-sannomiya and had a son, Kaoru. Genji had no choice but to accept the illegitimate son as his own and wondered if it was the result of his mistakes in his younger days. Finally, his loving Murasaki-no-ue passed away and the depressed Genji considered becoming a priest.

After Genji's death, the story continues in *Uji Jujo* (The Ten Chapters of Uji), which takes place in nearby Uji. The main characters are Genji's youngest son—actually a son of Kashiwagi—Kaoru, and his grandson, Niou-no-miya. While Kaoru was reserved, Niou-no-miya was passionate. They were close but also rivals in romance. The story portrays the tragic love of these two main characters.

Wakamurasaki, Tosa Mitsuoki, 17th century

GENJI: PICTURE SCROLLS AND JAPANESE ART

Painted hand scrolls, called *emakimono*, flourished in Japan from the 11th century to the 16th. Thought to have originated in India, the art form arrived in Japan via China sometime during the 6th and 7th centuries. The horizontal scrolls depicted illustrated narratives, with stories about battles, romance, folklore, the supernatural, and religion—indeed, emakimono played a role in spreading Buddhism throughout Japan.

Created by joining together several dozen pieces of paper (and occasionally silk), the scrolls were then attached to wooden dowels to be rolled up, secured with braided silk cord, and stored away. To read an emakimono, which combined illustrations with summarizing text, it would be opened to arm's length and viewed from right to left. These beautifully crafted tales, up to 40-feet long sometimes, depicted several scenes, and usually took up to three entire scrolls to tell one story.

The *Genji Monogatari Emaki*, the most widely known and discussed example of a painted hand scroll, took between 10 to 20 scrolls to tell all 54 chapters of *The Tale of Genji*. Sadly, only an estimated 15 percent of the original hand scroll remains. The Tokugawa Art Museum in Nagoya has three of the scrolls, and the Gotoh Museum in Tokyo has one. Designated National Treasures of Japan, the scrolls are so fragile that they normally are not shown in public, except for one week in November at the Tokugawa Museum.

Heian Jingu and Taihei-kaku

(weeping cherry tree) at the former site of the Konoe family mansion, located in the north of Kyoto Gosho, has inspired many poets.

Heian Jingu Shrine

While Kyoto Gosho is the site where the emperors actually resided, Heian Jingu Shrine is a copy of the emperors' residence, recreating the old image of the Heian period. Heian Jingu was built in 1895, commemorating 1,100 years since the founding of Heian-kyo. It honors Emperor Kammu, who established the capital in Kyoto, and Emperor Komei, the last emperor who resided in Kyoto. The shrine complex is a five-eighths' scale replica of the Chodoin, the palace's main hall, where the important events and daily administrative duties were performed.

Entering the Ohten-mon gate, there is an open space covered with white pebbles. The large red shrine behind it is the central building, Daigokuden. The corridors spread to right and left from here and there is an elegant shrine garden, Shin-en, in the back. This would be a perfect spot to

LADY MURASAKI & THE TALE OF GENJI

Kamigamo shrine and Kamo (Aoi) Matsuri

imagine how Hikaru Genji lived.

As it was built only 100 years or so ago, Heian Jingu appears more colorful compared to other older shrines and temples. There are many interesting places to see in the shrine garden. The area surrounding the Taihei-kaku (Hashidono) is especially beautiful. This covered bridge over the pond allows you to see a breathtaking view of the landscape when the red weeping cherry trees blossom in spring. The autumn foliage season and the snowy season also have their own beauty. It would be a great loss not to see this garden.

Kyoto's Three Great Festivals

Another popular time to visit is the Jidai Matsuri (Festival of the Ages) on October 22nd of each year. This festival includes a magnificent parade of people dressed in traditional costumes, recreating the history from the Heian period to the Edo period, when Kyoto was the capital of Japan. Each year a lady dressed as Murasaki Shikibu, the author of *The Tale of Genji*, strolls in this parade draped in layers of colorful kimonos.

Kuruma arasoi-zu byobu, by Kano Sanraku, 17c ; *Flame (Vengeful spirit of Miyasudokoro)*, Uemura Shoen, 1918

When it comes to festivals (*matsuri* in Japanese), the Kamo (Aoi) Matsuri should not be forgotten. Celebrated on May 15th, the festival goes back over 1,400 years and was one of the important national events of the Heian period.

During the festival, the emperor would visit the Shimogamo and Kamigamo shrines to pray for good harvests and peace for the nation, their spectacular pageantry entertaining the people of the town. *The Tale of Genji* depicts a scene from the festival day when the whole town was crowded with people. While the prince Genji was the main sight of the procession, his lawful wife, Aoi-no-ue, and his lover, Rokujo-no-miyasudokoro, fought over a spot for their oxcarts from which to view. Losing the competition and feeling ashamed, Rokujo-no-miyasudokoro held a grudge toward Aoi-no-ue; later, upon hearing the news of Aoi-no-ue's pregnancy with Genji, her jealous spirit would haunt Aoi-no-ue to her death.

The Kamo Matsuri is now called Aoi Matsuri because hollyhock (*aoi* in Japanese) leaves are used to decorate the bamboo blinds, crowns and ox carts. The world of

LADY MURASAKI & THE TALE OF GENJI

TRANSLATIONS IN MODERN LANGUAGE AND FOREIGN LANGUAGES, COMICS

The Tale of Genji was widely read among Heian nobilities. However, there were already many explanatory notes toward the end of Heian period, which explains that the novel was not an easy read even then. Needless to say, it is difficult to comprehend in the original language now. There have been various translations into modern Japanese since the Meiji period. The famous poet Yosano Akiko, literary legend Tanizaki Junichiro, and other well-known authors like Enchi Fumiko, Tanabe Seiko, Hashimoto Osamu, and Setouchi Jakucho, to name a few, have translated this novel—all became best sellers, thanks to Genji's timeless popular. Nonetheless, it is not easy to finish the entire novel and for many Japanese, it is a masterpiece that they would like to read someday but find hard to get started.

The Tale of Genji has been translated into over 20 foreign languages. There are several English translations, including those by Arthur David Waley, Edward George Seidensticker, and Royall Tyler.

The most widely read version of this novel in Japanese, however, could be *Asaki Yumemishi*, a manga (comic book). The author, Yamato Waki, read the original book thoroughly and faithfully recreated it into a manga for girls. She succeeded in visualizing the gorgeous lifestyle of Heian court culture and made the story appealing and easy to understand. You may call it a modern-day *Tale of Genji* picture scroll (*emaki*). The complicated relationships between the characters can be easily comprehended in this version. Setouchi Jakucho, one of the authors to the modern Japanese translation, praises this manga and says, "Yamato Waki is the 20th century Murasaki Shikibu. She could be the reincarnated Murasaki Shikibu."

Although this manga version of *The Tale of Genji* was published about 30 years ago, it has been continuously purchased and is regarded as a classic. Today, the total sales have reached approximately 18 million copies. Many high school students read this comic to understand the original novel to prepare for exams. It has been translated into foreign languages and has spread the story to wider audiences.

Genji from the *Asakiyumemishi* manga

MOVIES, PLAYS, ANIMATIONS

The Tale of Genji has become a popular theme of art including picture scrolls, craftworks, Noh plays and kabuki theater. In the 20th and 21st centuries, a variety of movies, plays, TV dramas, and animated films based on the story have been produced. Hikaru Genji is usually played by popular, good-looking actors or sometimes by actresses dressed as a handsome man. The recent movie The Tale of Genji—The Mystery of The Millennium was released in December 2011. It featured author Murasaki Shikibu as the main character, and portrayed the historical reality of her creating the novel with the imaginary world of the novel appearing at the same time.

TRADITIONAL EVENTS RELATED TO THE TALE OF GENJI

Many of the events in Heian court culture that we read about in The Tale of Genji have been passed down to our modern life as annual festivals like Aoi Matsuri. For instance, in the old lunar calendar, May was the season for long periods of rain when people needed to avoid getting pests and having food go rotten. People performed "Shobu no Sechie" where they tried to drive away negative spirits by using aromatic odor of plants like irises. This traditional event is now performed as "Tango no Sekku" on May 5th each year.

The Tale of Genji still lives in this festival. The procession starts from the palace at 10:30 a.m. and arrives at the Kamigamo Shrine at around 3:30 p.m., recreating the elegant Heian pageantry in the bright green of spring. The roadsides are crowded with the onlookers vying for good viewing spots, just like in the Heian period.

Together with the Gion Matsuri, which takes place throughout the month of July and culminates in a float-filled parade, the Jidai Matsuri and Aoi Matsuri are called Kyoto's Three Great Festivals.

Author Murasaki Shikibu

When The Tale of Genji was created, author Murasaki Shikibu was working for the young Empress Shoshi, who was a daughter of one of the most powerful nobles of the time, Fujiwara Michinaga. It was Michinaga who ordered Lady Murasaki to write a story in order to direct the Emperor Ichijo's attention to Shoshi. Lady Murasaki completed this lengthy novel under Michinaga's protection. As Michinaga expected, The Tale of Genji attracted the emperor, who loved literature, and Shoshi was blessed with two sons, who both later became emperors. Michinaga's own power increased in the meantime.

Murasaki Shikibu resided on the present site of Rozan-ji

Murasaki Shikibu was born into a middle-rank noble family that kept provincial government positions. While her mother passed away early, she was a talented child and her father, a well-known literary man, educated her. In her diary, *Murasaki Shikibu Nikki*, she boasted that she read Chinese classics, including *Shiki* (The Records of the Grand Historian), which were considered men's literature at the time; "What a shame. What if you were a man?" her father lamented.

Lady Murasaki married Yamashiro-no-kami—who was about twenty years older and already had a wife and family—after she had turned older than the typical wedding age. She had a daughter but her husband died from illness only three years after the marriage.

While she was from a middle-rank noble family, working for the Empress Shoshi exposed her to the lifestyle of the upper nobility and to the palace, and gave her the resources for writing *The Tale of Genji*. The story was so popular among the court ladies that they looked forward to each new part as she finished. The readers must have talked about the story both at work and home, making guesses as to who was the model for each character.

Similarities between womanizing Hikaru Genji and the image of Michinaga can certainly be found. As smart a lady as Lady Murasaki was, the powerful Michinaga must have been a target of examination and a resource for the novel. However, there is also a strong argument that she was one of his lovers.

WHERE TO SEE

❶ KYOTO GOSHO
京都御所

Subway to Karasuma-Imadegawa
Bus to Karasuma-Imadegawa
Imperial Household Agency Kyoto
Bureau: 075-211-1215
sankan.kunaicho.go.jp/english

This palace was home of the emperors for 500 years until Emperor Meiji moved the capital to Tokyo in 1869. The current building was built in 1855, following the Heian style. There is the Seiryoden, where the emperors would perform their daily duties, and the Shishinden, where the important ceremonies including the emperor's accession ceremony would be carried out. It is open to public during the periods in spring and fall; visitors are accepted by appointment during other times. English tours (about an hour) are available upon prior appointment. by phone or online. The palace is surrounded by a large park called Kyoto Gyoen, which is open to public.

❷ HEIAN JINGU SHRINE
平安神宮

Nishi Tenno-cho, Okazaki Sakyo-ku, Kyoto
www.heianjingu.or.jp/index_e.html

Heian Jingu was built in 1895, commemorating 1,100 years since the founding of the Heian capital. It is a replica of the Chodo-in, the main hall of the old Imperial Palace, in the scale of five-eighths of the original building. A huge, bright red torii gate stands over Jingu-do Street, marking the entrance to the sacred space of the Shinto shrine. The Shin-en (shrine garden) is well

Kyoto Gosho

LADY MURASAKI & THE TALE OF GENJI

Shimogamo Shrine

known for its cherry blossoms. There is a small admission fee for the garden. On October 22nd, the Festival of Ages, Jidai Matsuri, takes place here.

❸ KAMIGAMO SHRINE/
❹ SHIMOGAMO SHRINE—
UNESCO WORLD HERITAGE SITE
上賀茂神社／下鴨神社

339 Motoyama, Kamigamo, Kita-ku, Kyoto
www.kamigamojinja.jp/english/index.html

59 Shimogamo-izumigawa-cho,
Sakyo-ku, Kyoto
www.shimogamo-jinja.or.jp/english.
html

The Kamo River runs through Kyoto and Kamigamo Shrine is located at its upper reaches and Shimogamo Shrine at the lower reaches of the river. The two shrines are together called Kamosha. They are the oldest shrines in Kyoto; both are registered as UNESCO World Heritage sites. The successive emperors worshiped at these shrines to their guardian god, *ujigami*, and made offerings and prayers at times of national crisis. Aoi Matsuri, the shrines' annual festival, dates back as early as the 6th century and has always attracted crowds of onlookers since those early days. The official name of Kamigamo Shrine is Kamo-wake-ikazuchi Jinja; here the divine power of thunder (*ikazuchi*)

is believed to drive away bad luck and protect people from any disaster. The current shrine's foundation was built in 678. On the day of Tango-no-Sekku (the Boys' Festival), May 5th, the Kurabe-uma ritual is held where running horses are believed to chase away evil spirits.

Shimogamo Shrine hosts a traditional *kemari* event every January 4th. Kemari is a ball-passing game that originally came from China 1,400 years ago and became popular during the Heian period. In the annual kemari event, participants, dressed in the costumes of the Heian nobility, kick the ball in a graceful manner, softly trying to keep it afloat. The *yabusame* (mounted archery) ritual is held annually on May 3rd, when archers in traditional costume, mounted on galloping horses, shoot targets and reenact scenes of the time of *The Tale of the Genji*. People come to Aioi Shrine—a small shrine on the grounds of Shimogamo dedicated to the god of good marriage—to pick up a fortune slip based on lines from *The Tale of Genji*, hoping their union will fare better than the protagonist's.

KYOTO

Daikaku-ji

Shikibu is believed to have gotten the idea from the fact that Emperor Saga loved this location, away from the capital's center, and lived in seclusion here. It is home to the oldest manmade pond in Japan, Osawa Pond, a fine example of Heian gardening style. It is said that one of Japan's traditional flower arrangement schools, Ikebana Sagami-ryu, started when Emperor Saga picked chrysanthemum flowers in this palace's garden and arranged them in a pot.

❺ DAIKAKU-JI TEMPLE
大覚寺

4 Saga-osawa-cho, Ukyo-ku, Kyoto
www.daikakuji.or.jp/en
075-871-0071

Having lost his dear wife Murasaki-no-ue, the heartbroken Genji spent the rest of his life as a priest at Saga-no-in Temple, which is believed to have been modeled after Daikaku-ji. Daikaku-ji Temple was originally an imperial villa for Emperor Saga, successor of the founder of the Heian capital, Emperor Kammu. Murasaki

❻ SHOSEI-EN GARDEN
渉成園

Shomen-dori Aino-machi Higashi-iru,
Shimogyo-ku, Kyoto
www.higashihonganji.or.jp/english
075-75-371-9210

Shosei-en Garden

LADY MURASAKI & THE TALE OF GENJI

Shosei-en Gaden is a second residence of the Higashi-Hongan-ji Temple, also known as Kikoku-Tei, due to the fact that hardy orange trees (*karatachi* or *kikoku*) were planted at the hedges. It is known as the remaining site of Minister of the Left Minamoto-no-Toru's residence, Kawarano-in. He is believed to be one of the living models of Hikaru Genji.

Minamoto-no-Toru was an heir to Emperor Saga. Since the Emperor had 50 children and Minamoto-no-Toru's mother had lower status compared to other mothers, he received Minamoto as his surname and assumed a vassal's position with no chance to succeed the throne. However, he rose to become the Minister of the Left and enjoy prosperity. This background is very similar to that of Hikaru Genji. Minamoto-no-Toru built a large mansion, Kawarano-in, near Kamo River in Heian capital, and it is belived to be the model of Hikaru Genji's mansion, Rokujo-in, in *The Tale of Genji*. (Some believe that this is the model of Sono-in where Hikaru Genji took Yugao to.) However, geographically speaking, this site is a little away from Kawarano-in's site. Thus, it could be a folktale. Still, there is a memorial tower for Minamoto-no-Toru and the garden is full of the Heian court culture's atmosphere. It is an ideal site to experience the world of *The Tale of Genji*.

TASTY SPECIALTIES FOR VISITORS TO THE KAMO SHRINES

Shimogamo Shrine is also known for its beloved sweet, the *mitarashi dango* (sticky rice balls on stick, covered in sweet sauce). It is believed that the round shape of the dango mimicked the bubbles seen in the Mitarashi-no-Ike pond at the shrine. In the beginning, people started making these dangos as offerings to the shrine, wishing for the deity's protection for good health. Today, similar dangos are widely available in supermarkets and convenience stores alike, but people are fond of the taste of the original.

Kamigamo Shrine's specialty food is yakimochi, a toasted daifuku (sticky rice cake with sweet bean paste). There is always a line of customers who wish to taste the simple, traditional sweets. Some people believe that this cake is good for avoiding affairs because *yakimochi* also means "jealousy" in Japanese. Jinbado (Tel: 075-781-1377) is the most popular shop. They close when they sell out.

KYOTO

WHERE TO SEE

❼ ROSAN-JI TEMPLE-LADY MURASAKI'S RESIDENCE
蘆山寺

Hirokoji-agaru, Teramachi-dori, Kamigyo-ku, Kyoto

It is presumed that Murasaki Shikibu resided where the site of the Rozan-ji Temple is now. Located near Kyoto Gosho palace, the temple was transferred here in the late 16th century. During the Heian period, it is believed that Lady Murasaki's grandfather's residence was here and she grew up, spent her married life (it was the custom of this period that a husband joined his wife's family home), and wrote *The Tale of Genji* here. These historical facts were only discovered about 40 years ago. Since then, this temple has become known for its relationship to Lady Murasaki and its front garden has been called "Genji Garden."

Sitting at the veranda of the temple, gazing over the mossy garden in white sand, imagine Lady Murasaki pondering over the plot of her story, never knowing that people would keep reading her story for a millennium to come. June through September, the purple balloon flowers planted to commemorate Murasaki blossom softly. There is a monument to her poem in the temple grounds.

❽ URIN-IN TEMPLE
雲林院

Murasakino Urinin-cho, Kita-ku, Kyoto

Urin-in Temple is now a small temple, but it used to have much larger grounds and was very well known. Actually, the surrounding neighborhood is called Urinin-cho (town of Urin-in), which leads scholars to believe that this temple was sizable. Some argue that Murasaki Shikibu spent her last days here,

Rosan-ji and Lady Murasaki's tomb near Urin-in

LADY MURASAKI & THE TALE OF GENJI

Urin-in Temple

probably due to the fact that her grave is located not far from here, although there is no evidence to prove it. In *The Tale of Genji*, Hikaru Genji withdrew himself into this temple after being rejected by his stepmother Fujitsubo and feeling desperate.

❾ TRY ON HEIAN COURT COSTUMES AT HEIAN COSTUME EXPERIENCE STUDIO

58 Matsuya-cho, Nijo-dori,
Takakura-Nishi-iru, Nakagyo-ku, Kyoto
www.junihitoe.net (English)

Picture yourself in Genji's time by trying on the gorgeous costumes of the Heian period at this studio. The twelve-layered kimonos of the Heian court ladies are available here, as are the traditional court costumes that today's Imperial family wears at ceremonies like weddings. The modern Japanese do not wear kimonos very often, let alone twelve-layered kimonos, unless they are actors in historical dramas. And these costumes are not imitations for playful fun, but genuine high-quality Heian-style kimonos. You can choose the colors and patterns of your choice. Men may enjoy feeling like the dashing Hikaru Genji.

It takes two to three hours for make-up, dressing and photos (with your own camera) and the fees start at 20,000 yen and up for both women and men. The fees are based on your choice of costumes; the fee for the most expensive twelve-layered kimono is 280,000 yen. A professional photographer can be arranged for a separate charge.

宇治

UJI

Statue of Murasaki Shikibu at Uji-bashi

The Tale of Genji and the Heian Picture Scrolls: Uji

The latter half of *The Tale of Genji* takes place in the town of Uji, located on the southern outskirts of Kyoto. After Hikaru Genji passed away, the story follows his youngest son, Kaoru, and his grandson, Nio-no-Miya, on their own tragic romances. It is as if spring turns to fall and day becomes evening. Some researchers claim that *Uji Jujo* was written by someone other than Murasaki Shikibu, possibly even a man. However, the belief that Lady Murasaki is the author is widely accepted.

Uji was blessed with nature's beauty and Heian aristocrats preferred to have their villas there. Minamoto-no-Toru, who is believed to be a model for Hikaru Genji, and Fujiwara Michinaga, Lady Murasaki's patron, had villas in Uji, where they enjoyed taking their boats out and viewing the autumn foliage. Lady Murasaki would have likely accompanied Empress Shoshi on visits to Uji and gained ideas for the story.

Uji was the type of place where the Heian nobility could have felt a solemn peace in their souls. You can get glimpses of the Buddhist's view of the world, with its emphasis on the transience of human life, throughout the ten chapters of *Uji Jujo*.

Starting with "Hashi Hime" (bridge princess) and ending with "Yume-no-uki-hashi" (floating bridge of dreams), the mist-covered Uji River and bridge are the important and evocative motifs throughout the tale. The bridge, which connects the two parts of the story, also represents the connection between this world and the other world, as well as the connection between men and women. With this image of the bridge, let's leave Kyoto city behind and extend our visit to Uji.

Visiting Uji

Hopping onto a JR rapid train at Kyoto Station, you can get to Uji in 17 minutes. Even though Uji has been talked about in numerous literary works, including *Man-yo-shu* ("The Anthology of Myriad Leaves") and *The Tale of Heike*, for its beautiful scenery, not that many people

Miryu Bridge

LADY MURASAKI & THE TALE OF GENJI

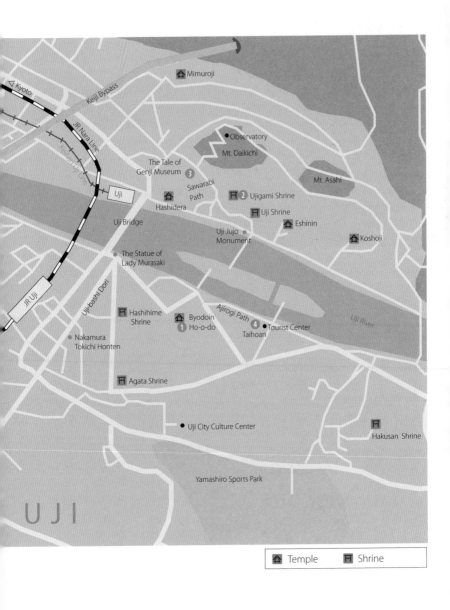

◁ Kyoto

Keiji Bypass

JR Nara Line

Keihan Uji Line

Mimuroji

Uji

● Observatory
Mt. Daikichi

The Tale of
Genji Museum ③

Sawarabi Path

Mt. Asahi

🈁 ② Ujigami Shrine

Hashidera

🈁 Uji Shrine

Uji Bridge

Eshinin

Uji Jujo Monument

Koshoji

The Statue of
Lady Murasaki

JR Uji

Uji-bashi Dori

Hashihime Shrine

Ajirogi Path

Byodoin
① Ho-o-do

④ Tourist Center
Taihoan

Uji River

● Nakamura
Tokichi Honten

Agata Shrine

Uji City Culture Center

Hakusan Shrine

Yamashiro Sports Park

U J I

🏯 Temple	🈁 Shrine

The view from Uji-bashi

come to visit. It could be because it is not well known compared to the more famous sightseeing spots in Kyoto, or that it seems far away although it is not. Uji is a nice place to visit without the rush and the crowds.

There is an old bridge crossing over Uji River called Uji-bashi, originally built in 646. The view of this bridge from upstream, together with the clear water and somber mountains in the background, is magnificent.

There is a statute of Murasaki Shikibu at the foot of Uji Bridge, and a monument of a scene from *Uji Jujo* is at the other side. Recently, Uji-city has been trying to attract tourists as the "Town of The Tale of Genji."

There are many spots of historical interest related to the Heian period for tourists and Genji fans alike.

Byodo-in Temple's Ho-o-do (Phoenix Hall, a UNSECO World Heritage Site) is the city's must-see spot. If you have a ten-yen coin, flip it around to see the picture on the back: Phoenix Hall. This hall dedicated to the Amida

Azumaya scene from *Genji Monogatari Emaki*, 12c., Tokugawa Art Museum

Buddha has transepts to its left and right, and it seems just like a phoenix spreading its wings. The image reflecting on the pond is also breathtakingly beautiful. There is a 280-year-old wisteria tree, which has gorgeous flowers blooming on a trellis during the spring. The purple wisteria flowers fit perfectly with the elegance of Heian culture.

Byodo-in Temple was created by Fujiwara Yorimichi, the chief advisor to the emperors, in 1052, by remodeling the resort house that he inherited from his father, Michinaga, who was the most powerful and influential political noble of that time. Phoenix Hall was built the following year, 1053. This elegant hall was to represent the image of heaven and still captivates its visitors today. It is believed that the entire garden—with the Uji River and the mountains in the background—was built as an earthly replica of pure land, the Buddhist image of heaven.

It is almost a miracle that the temple hall and statues of the Buddha from around 1,000 years ago have survived fires and bombings and still stand in front of us today.

Byodo-in Temple's Ho-o-do (Phoenix Hall)

In comparison, the Muryoko-in Temple of Hiraizumi in Tohoku, which was modeled after Phoenix Hall, has long been burnt down to only remains in a bleak field.

It is said that Minamoto-no-Toru had his resort house on the Byodo-in site. In *Uji Jujo*, Nio-no-miya visits Yugiri, Hikaru Genji's son, at his resort villa in Uji. It is believed that Yugiri's villa was modeled on this temple.

In this villa, Nio-no-miya and his guests would play music—the sound of which traveled over the Uji River to reach the mountain villa of Hachino-miya, Genji's half brother, whose daughters had relationships with both Kaoru and Nio-no-miya. The model for Hachino-miya's mountain villa is believed to be the Ujigami Shrine.

The altar hall at Ujigami Shrine is made in the simple yet tasteful style of a Heian aristocrat's residence. The main hall was made in the Heian period and is known as the oldest shrine building in Japan. It is rather a quiet, small shrine blending in with the trees in the back, but it is registered among the UNESCO World

LADY MURASAKI & THE TALE OF GENJI

Ujigami Shrine and its main hall (right)

Heritage sites of ancient Kyoto.

The locations of the Byodo-in Temple and Ujigami Shrine are exactly the same as the two villas in *Uji Jujo*. The atmosphere of this place fits perfectly to the story setting where the prince, lamenting his ill fate in the capital's politics, hides out with the princesses. You can imagine hearing the rustling sound of their silk kimonos behind the bamboo blinds.

From Ujigami Shrine, you can walk on a cobblestone trail called Sawarabi-no-Michi (Early Ferns, after the name of a chapter in *The Tale of Genji*) to The Tale of Genji Museum, which explains the world of the novel and the court culture of the time in an easy to understand manner. There is a model of Rokujo-in—Genji's residence, which was supposed to be about double the size of a baseball field—costumes and furnishings of the time, and a theater where you can see a movie of some well-known scenes from *Uji Jujo*. The museum offers a good background on the story that would be helpful before visiting the sightseeing spots associated with the novel.

Uji Jujo monument and historic site of Uji Jujo (Ukifune)

The most notable item in this museum is a restored oxcart, which is lacquered to a gloss and larger and higher than would be expected—nobles in the Heian period would use stepstools in order to get on it. It must have been even more impressive to see an oxcart on the main avenue to the court, Suzaku-dori, than to see a stretch limousine on Manhattan's Fifth Avenue today.

Another must-see is the exhibition of Heian incense culture, which was an important part of the lives of the nobility.

In *The Tale of Genji*, incense is an indispensable element for portraying each character and scene. The fragrances that Heian nobles used had different aromas from the perfumes of the west, such as sandalwood or aloeswood. The nobles would blend their own incense and burn it to infuse the smell into their clothing and into letters depending on the occasion. The fragrances were part of their self-expression.

Actually, the name of one character, Kaoru, means "scent," and the name of another, Nio-no-miya, means "prince of fragrance." You can smell the sample incenses at this museum and create in your own imagination the fragrances of the characters.

LADY MURASAKI & THE TALE OF GENJI

The Tale of Genji Museum

Uji Tea

Some people think of green tea when hearing the name Uji, for it is a famous green-tea-producing region in Japan. They say that the mist from the Uji River protects the tea leaves and makes them a fine quality. Uji tea is synonymous high quality.

Tea was introduced to Japan by China in the 13th century during the Kamakura period, so it was not yet known at the time of *The Tale of Genji*. During Muromachi period, which lasted from the 14th through the 16th century, the Japanese started growing tea themselves. Warlords Oda Nobunaga and Toyotomi Hideyoshi supported protected the growers. As Nobunaga and Hideyoshi were patrons of the tea ceremony and made it very popular, the reputation of Uji tea grew with it. Even after the center of politics moved from Kyoto to Tokyo (Edo) during the Edo period, Uji tea growers remained the suppliers to the shogun family and they have kept up the reputation of high-quality tea even to this day.

Uji's natural beauty and clean water, as well as its strong aesthetic sense, have endured for over 1,000 years,

Miss Uji Tea ladies in the tea fields

sustaining its tea culture and influencing the way tea is enjoyed all throughout Japan. For example, the name of the popular Japanese dessert, *uji kintoki*, means *matcha* (fine powdered tea) and red beans—with the word *uji* used as a synonym for green tea.

You will find many tea shops along the streets in this city. Uji's tea tastes mild and subtly sweet. (Naturally, locals do not add any sweeteners.) Some shops even offer free tastings.

Besides green tea, these shops also make sweets such as cake rolls and cheesecakes with Uji matcha. It is a good idea to stop by a café serving matcha and sweets to take a break from sightseeing. Nakamura Tokichi Honten is a quaint old shop and worth visiting at least to see the building.

There are facilities where you can learn how to brew tasty tea, experience the tea ceremony in a casual manner, or see materials having to do with tea

Nakamura Tokichi Honten, matcha tea
and green tea parfait

manufacturing. Even for those who have had only tea
from a bottle or teabag, it is a good opportunity to
discover the world of tea.

While enjoying aromatic Uji green tea, you can
discover the city's charm, which is a little different from
that of central Kyoto, and experience the melancholy
world of *Uji Jujo*.

❶ BYODO-IN HO-O-DO (PHOENIX HALL)—
UNESCO WORLD HERITAGE SITE
平等院・鳳凰堂

116 Uji-renge, Uji
www.byodoin.or.jp/english.html

Fujiwara Yorimichi, the chief advisor to the emperor, inherited this vacation home from his father, Michinaga, in 1052 and remodeled it to a temple. Phoenix Hall was built in the following year and is home to a statue of the Amida Buddha. Its large roof is decorated with a statute of a phoenix and the interior is brightly painted with angels dancing and playing music, as well as phoenixes taking wing. An additional 52 *Unchu-kuyo bodhisattva* (wooden worshiping bodhisattvas on clouds) statutes hang on the walls, playing music and dancing on clouds. The double-layered golden canopy is also magnificent. There are 66 copper mirrors hanging from the ceiling to reflect the candlelight during

the night, transforming the space into a world of fantasy. It is as gorgeous as the sight of the Buddhist pure land, the celestial realm of enlightenment. Since 2001, a museum, Hosho-kan, has displayed historic treasures associated with the temple.

❷ UJIGAMI SHRINE—
UNESCO WORLD HERITAGE SITE
宇治上神社

59 Uji-yamada, Uji
0774-21-4634

Ujigami enshrines Emperor Ojin, his prince, Ujino-waki-iratsuko, and his older brother, Emperor Nintoku. Until the Meiji period, this shrine was combined with the neighboring Uji Shrine and called Riku Kamisha. The altar hall was built in the beginning of the Kamakura period in the style of a Heian noble's residence. The main hall was built in the late Heian period and believed to be the oldest shrine building in Japan. There is a spring called Kirihara-mizu in the grounds of this shrine, which is noted as one of Uji's seven best water sources. However, since the other six water sources have dried out, this is the last famous water

Ujigami Shrine

LADY MURASAKI & THE TALE OF GENJI

in Uji. (Be aware that you have to boil it before drinking.) Because Uji used to be written in Chinese characters meaning "Rabbit Road," you will find rabbits as a motif throughout the shrine. Pick a written oracle by choosing one of the cute, colorful rabbit dolls.

❸ THE TALE OF GENJI MUSEUM
源氏物語ミュージアム

45–26 Uji-Higashiuchi, Uji
www.uji-genji.jp/en/

Visitors can have fun and learn about the world of *The Tale of Genji* and Heian culture at this museum, with exhibits on Heian clothing, incense and more. The documents and materials regarding *The Tale of Genji* are housed in a library. You can also view a movie *Hashi-hime*, which shows the perspectives of the world of *Uji Jujo* in just 20 minutes.

Tea house Taiho-an

❹ TEA HOUSE TAIHO-AN
茶室「対凰庵」

1–5 Uji Togawa, Uji
Uji-City Tourism Center
0774-23-3334

This facility was established for promoting Uji tea and the tea ceremony. Taiho-an literally means "facing Phoenix House" because of its location across from the Phoenix Hall. In this authentic tea house, visitors can drink genuine Uji green tea in the traditional tea ceremony. Chairs are also available for those who prefer not to sit on the floor for the ceremony. Tickets for participating in the ceremony with seasonal sweets are sold at Uji-City Tourism Center, which is next door to this tea house.

e Tale of Genji Museum

織田信長
ODA NOBUNAGA

Wooden statue of Nobunaga at Daitoku-ji Soken-in, 1583

Oda Nobunaga, The Warlord Who Won the Sengoku Period with Guns and Tea

Kyoto was burned down several times during the ten years of the Onin War (1467–1477), a period when the city experienced rampant destruction and robbery and many of the cultural properties inherited from the Heian period were lost. The effect of the war was so severe that some argue that Japan's culture was reset: The glamorous Heian culture, with its East Asian and Middle Eastern influences, was replaced by a uniquely Japanese culture valuing simplicity.

The era of leader Oda Nobunaga came 100 years after this cultural transformation, at the time when Christian missionaries arrived from Portugal and Spain, and Japan started absorbing European culture.

In 1549, the Spanish missionary Francisco Xavier came to Japan and introduced Christianity. After that, Jesuit missionaries came, one after another, and further promoted Christianity and Western culture in Japan.

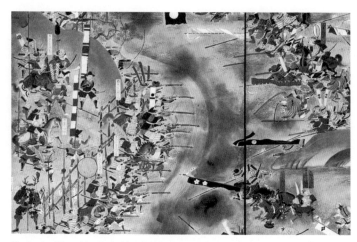

The Battle of Nagashino Byobu (detail), 18th century, Tokugawa Art Museum

Nobunaga (1534–1582) would be the first leader in Japanese history to promote trading with Europe in earnest and welcome Western culture.

Rising among the warlords of the Sengoku (Warring States) period, which lasted between the late 15th century and early 17th century, when a number of warlords rose to power and competed against each other to rule the country, Nobunaga fought his way toward unifying Japan and almost succeeded in his dream.

Although Nobunaga is not well known outside of Japan, he had an immense impact on Japan's history, by opening its doors to the modern age, thanks, in part, to his appreciation for the culture brought from the West.

Nobunaga had carefully calculated political intentions as he embraced European culture by wearing a cloak and drinking wine. For one thing, promoting trade with Europe and protecting Christianity was useful in suppressing the rising power of the Buddhists on the political stage at the time.

ODA NOBUNAGA

LIFE OF ODA NOBUNAGA

Oda Nobunaga was born on May 12, Tenmon 3 (June 23, 1534). He was given the castle of Nagoya by his father, Oda Nobuhide, and became a lord when he was only 2 years old. After his father passed away, he succeeded as ruler of the Oda clan at the age of 18. Even though he was called a fool and people worried about his future when he was a young boy, he gradually displayed his capabilities as a warrior and came to unite the Owari region (the western part of Aichi Prefecture). In 1560, he made a bold ambush to defeat the large army of Imagawa Yoshimoto at the battle of Okehazama—where no one imagined that Nobunaga could possibly win—and became a contender toward unifying Japan.

He then won the region of Mino (around Gifu Prefecture). Nobunaga was exceptionally strong in battle and was generally known for his cruel personality, described in the famous haiku: "If a bird doesn't sing, kill it." He started using Tenka Fubu as his seal, which represented his will to destroy all enemies through military power in order to unite the country. In 1568, he went into the capital with his troops in support of Ashikaga Yoshiaki, who became the 15th shogun. He gained enormous power, including the support from the rich Sakai merchants. However, just before his dream could come true, he was attacked in a rebellion led by his general, Akechi Mitsuhide.

On June 2, Tensho 10 (June 21, 1582), Nobunaga committed suicide while under siege by Mitsuhide's men in Honno-ji Temple without accomplishing his dream of unifying Japan under a single leader. He was just short of 50 years old. It was like a passage from *Atsumori*, one of the Kowaka-mai dance repertoires, which he liked and danced often: "Fifty years of human life is just like a day in heaven. Every life must perish in the end. For the life is so fragile and short, live all your dreams without fearing death."

NOBUNAGA CHRONOLOGY

1534: Born as a son of Oda Nobuhide in the Owari region

1551: Became the head of Oda clan

1560: Defeated the Imagawa Yoshimoto at the battle of Okehazama

1568: Entered the capital, supporting Ashikaga Yoshiaki

1570: Defeated the alliance of the Asai and Asakura clans at the Battle of Anegawa

1571: Burnt down the Hieizan Enryaku-ji Temple

1573: Ousted Ashikaga Yoshiaki, ending the Muromachi shogunate

1575: Defeated the Takeda clan at the Battle of Nagashino; suppressed the Echizen Ikko-Ikki peasant uprising

1576: Started building Azuchi castle. The castle tower was completed in 1579.

1582: Incident at Honno-ji Temple: Nobunaga committed suicide due to the rebellion of Akechi Mitsuhide

ONIN WAR

The Onin War, a civil war that lasted 10 years, resulted in the destruction of Kyoto, the end of the Ashikaga shogunate, and it marked the beginning of the Sengoku Jidai, a period of 100 years of strife and feuding.

The conflict began when shogun Ashikaga Yoshimasa, who had not had a son, convinced his brother to leave the monastery and become heir apparent. However, soon after, Ashikaga's wife bore him a son, and Ashikaga set about to undo his actions and name his son rightful heir.

The prime minister of the Ashikaga shogunate, Hosokawa Katsumoto, sided with Yoshimi, the brother. Meanwhile, Yamane Mochitoyo, whose family included powerful landowners, favored the son.

Warfare erupted between the sides, which had each raised considerable armies. Fighting only ceased because of pure exhaustion and fatigue. Feuding continued for 100 years, until the country was unified under Toyotomi Hideyoshi.

A Jesuit missionary, Luís Froís, arrived Japan in 1563 at the age of 31. He kept detailed notes and passed them to the missionaries who followed to pursue the propagation of Christianity in Japan. This huge record is called *History of Japan* and is important material for studying the Warring States Period in Japan. In the book, Froís described Nobunaga as follows:

"Nobunaga is tall, skinny, thin-bearded, and has a high voice. Although he is crude and likes martial arts, he also acts with justice and mercy. A sharp decision maker who does not rely on his subordinates but keeps his decisions to himself."

Froís must have perceived Nobunaga's talent as a leader.

It is difficult to describe Nobunaga's allure in a sentence or two. Accounts recall an unconventional personality. Although he was born an heir to a lord in the Owari region (near the present-day city of Nagoya), he was called a fool as a child because he always dressed and acted sloppily. However, as he grew older, he became a military genius, stunning the nation by defeating a large enemy force of 25,000 (or 45,000 in another version of the story) with a mere 2,000 in his own army in the famous Battle of Okehazama. His life is filled

ODA NOBUNAGA

with such legends that have made him a dramatic hero.

At a time when the social order and people's status were strictly valued, Nobunaga behaved outrageously to the nobles and promoted anyone according to their talent regardless of their rank. He must have stood out conspicuously walking around in a velvet cloak from Europe, among the feudal warlords in kimonos.

He stood out in battle, too. He was the first to introduce firearms to the battlefield and created epoch-making military strategies, using massive guns against his enemies' swords and bows and drastically changing the traditional methods of battle at the time.

In order to promote economic growth, he broke with many restrictions, allowing more freedom for commercial activities within his territory through the creation of the *Rakuichi Rakuza*, free market and

Nanban Byobu (detail), by Kano Naizen, Momoyama period, Kobe City Museum

Myokaku-ji

guilds, and abolishing checkpoints so merchants could travel more easily. In short, he pushed through reforms by deregulation and taking power away from vested interests.

It was a turbulent period where battles were perpetually fought, but a few warlords wished to rule by intelligence and culture, not only by military power. Nobunaga was one of them. And even though it is not generally discussed in the history of Japan, Nobunaga put enormous efforts into cultural activities and tried to use them politically. He was a man of refined taste, who cherished poems and the tea ceremony.

Nobunaga and the Tea Ceremony

Nobunaga's interest in the tea ceremony, *cha-no-yu*, was outstanding. He was particularly eager to collect masterwork tea utensils: bowls, scoops, and caddies. He searched for top-notch collector's items regardless of price, calling his pursuit "*meibutsu-gari*" or "masterpiece hunting." Nobunaga had almost united Japan and did not feel the need for more money or rice land. Instead, he craved the masterpieces of the nation as a symbol of his power.

ODA NOBUNAGA

A portrait of Sen-no-Rikyu; *Onjoji* (flower vase), Sen-no-Rikyu, 1590

He obtained rare art pieces that no amount of money could buy by using his political power to convince the rich merchants who owned them give them away as gifts for him. Nobunaga, then, would throw large tea ceremonies to show off his collection and make people recognize his authority.

Nobunaga held his tea ceremonies at the Myokaku-ji and Shokoku-ji temples in Kyoto. He stayed at these temples when he visited the capital, and held tea ceremonies there for the rich merchants of Sakai (near Osaka), the commercial capital at the time.

Myokaku-ji Temple is about a 10-minute walk to the west from Kurama-guchi Station of the Karasuma subway line. This temple's garden is a great place to view the cherry blossoms in spring and also the fall foliage; not many people know about it. While this temple is associated with Nobunaga and his father-in-law, Saito Dosan, the current temple building is not the one where he actually stayed. It used to be around the Nijo-dori, a little bit more south than its current location. The original building no longer exists. Large tea ceremony events were held sometimes at Myokaku-ji. Records show Nobunaga hosted the one here, using *meibutsu*, the highest-valued utensils.

Sen-no-Rikyu, who established the *wabi-cha* style tea ceremony emphasizing simplicity, was a master of the ceremony.

In November 1573, Nobunaga held a large tea ceremony to welcome the rich Sakai merchants, including Tsuda Sokyu—who, like Rikyu, was known as one of the three great tea masters—and showed off his collection of *meibutsu*, while he served an exquisite full-course meal.

Today, a multi-course *kaiseki*-style meal is considered Japanese fine dining, but it was originally served at tea ceremonies. Every process of the event, including setting up the room with art and flowers, tea utensils, meal and service, is the expression of beauty and philosophy of the tea ceremony.

Nobunaga himself served the guests with exceptional manners, such as pouring sake and refilling rice bowls for them. It was unthinkable at the time that a warlord would serve sake to merchants.

While Nobunaga was a feared dictator who would kill anyone without hesitation, he also played the role of

a dedicated host, paying scrupulous attention to his guests and serving sumptuous dishes. He must have wanted the connection and support of those rich Sakai merchants, who could supply the weapons, like guns and gunpowder, which he needed.

A kaiseki-style meal

ODA NOBUNAGA

In the meantime, he displayed the masterpiece tea utensils that he made merchants offer him, a symbol of his power and political muscle capable of driving the merchants into submission.

Shokoku-ji and Jotenkaku Museum

Shokoku-ji Temple, where Nobunaga also stayed, still owns a large estate and remains busy with visitors. Originally erected in 1392 by Ashikaga Yoshimitsu, the third Muromachi shogun, Shokoku-ji Temple is in the center of Kyoto, both geographically and culturally.

To reach the south gate of this temple, go directly north from Imadegawa-gomon gate of Kyoto Gosho palace. Shokoku-ji's Hatto (Dharma Hall), features a famous ceiling painting called *Naki-ryu* (Howling Dragon). Featuring a fierce dragon, it was painted by Kano Mitsunobu when the building was reconstructed in 1605—23 years after Nobunaga's death. The name of the painting comes from the fact that when you stand under it and clap your hands, the echo sounds as if a dragon is howling. There are always visitors looking up the ceiling, clapping their hands to hear the dragon's howl.

THE MOST BELOVED HERO, NOBUNAGA

Nobunaga is an especially beloved historical figure and there have been uncountable novels, movies, TV dramas, manga comics, and games featuring him as the main character. Unlike other warlords of the Warring States Period, he boasted talent as a social innovator, superb artistic tastes, and his flexible mind and vision in accepting Western culture. Such progressive characteristics might account for his enduring popularity.

Interestingly, whenever the social paradigm is shifting a great deal and values are changing, just like now, Japanese return to Nobunaga's life story. Recently, new studies and discoveries, which overturn the conventional cruel image of Nobunaga, have been found. History textbooks might be rewritten in the near future.

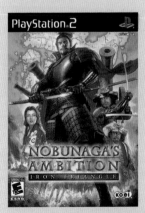

Nobunaga's Ambition video game

Shokoku-ji

Another popular spot at Shokoku-ji is the Jotenkaku
Museum. While it is rare to have a museum within
a temple's grounds, Shokoku-ji Temple produced
the artist Sesshu and other great Japanese ink-
painting artists. The museum exhibits many cultural
properties such as Zen-style calligraphy and paintings
from medieval to modern times, as well as tea
ceremony utensils like a bamboo teaspoon carved by
Sen-no-Rikyu himself. Most popular is the collection of
paintings by Ito Jakuchu, a prodigy in Kyoto art circles
in the 18th century.

Since the Meiji period, Jakuchu had been forgotten in
Japan. However, Joe Price, an American collector of
Edo-period paintings, brought his work back to Japan.
Ever since, Jakuchu's art has become so popular—
especially among the young generation—that there are
often long lines to see his exhibitions.

ODA NOBUNAGA

Meibutsu: Masterpiece Tea Utensils

Today, *meibutsu* are owned by museums. Nobunaga, however, not only cherished them as a collector, he used them to show off his power, and also gave them, along with the permission to hold tea ceremonies using them, as rewards to his vassals. Some vassals wished for tea utensils rather than new territories as their rewards.

While such utensils were considered masterpieces, they were not decorated with gorgeous gold leaf or precious gems. To untrained eyes, a tea case or bowl appears to be just a plain, humble container.

An Italian Jesuit missionary supervisor, Alessandro Valignano, who came to Japan three times in the 16th century, said of one of meibutsu, "it is totally unbelievable just how much appreciated these tools are. It is the kind of thing that only the Japanese would understand."

Nobunaga once told an opposing warlord to surrender: "Submit your tea ceremony kettle, and I'll spare your life." The opponent refused Nobunaga's offer and filled the kettle with gunpowder in order to die in the explosion—the tea kettle was a treasure for the warlord, which was worth his life.

MUSEUMS HOLDING NOBUNAGA'S MASTERPIECES

Ao Ido Chawan and *Tsukumo-nasu*

The famous *Ao Ido Chawan* (blue Ido-type tea bowl) that Nobunaga gave to his close vassal, Shibata Katsuie, is housed in the Nezu Museum in Aoyama, Tokyo. The name came from the fact that its glaze appears partly bluish ("*ao*"). Its inscription says "Shibata." It is a masterpiece tea bowl with a simple, rugged style.

A tea container made between the 12th and 13th centuries in China called *Tsukumo-nasu* is considered the greatest masterpiece of the Warring States Period. The round, eggplant ("*nasu*") -colored jar was in the possession of shogun Ashikaga Yoshimitsu before Nobunaga, and then passed onto Hideyoshi, Ieyasu and so on. It is currently housed in Seikado-bunko Museum in Setagaya, Tokyo. These famous tea utensils are not always on display, but available for viewing during special exhibitions.

NEZU ART MUSEUM
www.nezu-muse.or.jp/en

SEIKADO-BUNKO MUSEUM
www.seikado.or.jp/en

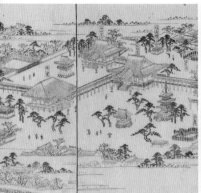

Honno-ji, 1780 (after the Incident of Honno-ji); Honno-ji today

Nobunaga's use of power to acquire his collection of masterpieces was mocked as "masterpiece hunting." However, he was not obsessed with their value only. It is apparent that he made decisions about what to collect based on his philosophy and sense of beauty.

The Incident at Honno-ji

In 1582, Nobunaga was killed in what is referred to as the Incident at Honno-ji, when his vassal, Akechi Mitsuhide, made a surprise attack. Nobunaga only had a few men with him and could not hold out. It is thought that he set fire to the temple and committed suicide, but his remains were never found.

Nobunaga had hosted a tea ceremony at Honno-ji Temple the day before he was attacked, and many of his priceless utensils were burned to ashes along with him. It is believed that one of Nobunga's leading vassals, Toyotomi Hideyoshi, dug up and recovered some of the masterpieces from the ashes.

Nobunaga's disappointing end came at the age of 49, when he was closing in on his goal of unifying Japan.

ODA NOBUNAGA

RANJATAI AND NOBUNAGA

It was not only tea utensils that Nobunaga used to show off his power. In 1574, Nobunaga boldly asked the emperor and the other imperial families for their famous aromatic wood, Ranjatai, which was kept in the Shoso-in* warehouse of the Todai-ji Temple in Nara. To display his power and prestige all over the country, Nobunaga knew, nothing is quite as good as using the authority of the emperor.

Ranjatai is a piece of aromatic agarwood, which has been kept in the Shoso-in warehouse since around 9th century, and is a hidden national treasure. It is longer than 60 in (150 cm) and is 8 to 16.5 in (21 to 42 cm) in diameter, weighing 25.5 lbs (11.6 kg), and it is said to start emitting an aroma with just a little heating. It is such a legendary aroma that only the Heian-period warrior-poet Minamoto Yorimasa and shogun Ashikaga Yoshimasa had had been given pieces of it in the entire history before Nobunaga. In Ashikaga Yoshimasa's case, it was not even officially given; he took it by force.

Nobunaga daringly asked for the emperor's permission and made the Shoso-in warehouse's door be opened for him. On March 28, he cut off a piece (approximately 2 in or 5.5 cm) of Ranjatai and left Nara in early on the morning of April 1st. Three days later, he held a tea ceremony at the Shokoku-ji Temple and showed off this precious aromatic wood, placed small pieces of it on a fan gracefully, and gave them to Tsuda Sokyu, a rich Sakai merchant, and Sen-no-Rikyu.

No matter how much economic power those rich merchants could have, receiving a royal treasure kept in the Shoso-in was unthinkable to a commoner. Nobunaga used this political display to bring the Sakai merchants to their knees, and strongly impressed people that he was indeed the ruler of the country. In a turbulent period where the warlords were fighting with each other to the death, how elegant that incense and tea utensils played such an important role. You may

wonder what the aroma Ranjatai is like. It is a piece of agarwood, a high-quality aromatic evergreen tree native to Southeast Asia, that has been infected with a particular type of mold. Ranjatai's aroma probably is like the highest quality agarwood, called *kyara*, eaglewood: deep, bitter but gracefully balanced fragrance. Eaglewood is now listed as a potentially threatened species by the Washington Convention after indiscriminate logging for this source of aroma. High-quality agarwood incense is commercially available in a stick form, but is very expensive.

---

*Shoso-in is a treasure house, which holds many fine arts and crafts from the 8th to the 10th century, including the emperors' favorite articles. It is located on the grounds of the Todai-ji Temple in Nara, which is famous for its Great Buddha.

AFTER NOBUNAGA: THE END OF AKECHI MITSUHIDE AFTER THE INCIDENT AT HONNO-JI

Hideyoshi

When Akechi Mitsuhide attacked Oda Nobunaga at Honno-ji Temple, Nobunaga's heir, Oda Nobutada, was staying less than a mile away at Myokaku-ji Temple. After Nobunaga killed himself, Mitsuhide went directly to Myokaku-ji, where Nobutada stayed. Nobutada, having heard of what happened at Honno-ji, had already moved to Nijo-gosho, but Mitsuhide's army came after him. Nobutada set fire to Nijo-gosho and killed himself.

While Mitsuhide got rid of Nobunaga in the surprise attack and changed the tide of history, he could not achieve his desire to be the ultimate leader. The vassal Hideyoshi hurried back to Kyoto and attacked Mitsuhide. As a result, Hideyoshi became the leading candidate to be Nobunaga's successor. Hideyoshi defeated Shibata Katsuie and other powerful vassals of Nobunaga, then finally united Japan in 1590.

When Hideyoshi became the ruler, he followed Nobunaga's interest in the tea ceremony. Unfortunately, Hideyoshi did not seem to have the same level of superior taste and sense of beauty. After he died in 1598, Tokugawa Ieyasu defeated the Toyotomi clan, and the Edo period began.

Nobunaga's loyal vassal Hideyoshi, in turn, attacked the traitor Mitsuhide and forced him to kill himself. Hideyoshi accomplished the unification of Japan that Nobunaga had fought for, and became the winner of the Warring States period.

Honno-ji still exists in Kyoto today, though it has moved and the huge estate and buildings have been lost to time. The "the solid structure like that of a castle, surrounded by high walls and a moat," described in records is not there any more. Its current main hall was rebuilt in 1928 after repeatedly being burnt down and rebuilt.

Because of its association with Nobunaga, the current Honno-ji has a memorial tower for the fallen leader within its grounds and displays his mementos and other related articles, such as his vassals' armor, in its museum. To pay tribute to Nobunaga in Kyoto, it might be better idea to visit Soken-in, one of Daitoku-ji's sub-temples.

Hideyoshi built Soken-in in order to console the spirit of his master, Nobunaga. Hideyoshi held a grand memorial service for Nobunaga here; graves for Nobunaga's family have been also established alongside his. Perhaps, Hideyoshi meant to

Soken-in (clockwise from top): the original main gate from 1583; the Oda family's gravesite; the tea ceremony room at Soken-in

show that he was going to be Nobunaga's successor by presiding over Nobunaga's funeral.

Since Nobunaga's body has never been found, no true grave exists. However, there are about 20 memorial towers for Nobunaga throughout Japan, including Soken-in, Honno-ji, Amida-dera—which claims to have Nobunaga's true grave—and Azuchi Castle.

The Soken-in Temple has three tea ceremony rooms, which were probably aligned with Nobunaga's tastes. Tea ceremony culture was passed onto Hideyoshi, who also held large tea ceremonies there. Under his rule, the art form of *cha-no-yu* fully blossomed during the Momoyama period.

WHERE TO SEE

❶ SHOKOKU-JI TEMPLE
相国寺

Karasuma Higashi-iru, Imadegawa-dori,
Kamigyo-ku, Kyoto
www.shokoku-ji.jp

Shokoku-ji is the national headquarters of the Rinzai-sect Shokoku-ji School. The principal object of worship is Shaka, the Buddha, Siddhartha Gautama. It was established in 1392 by the third shogun of the Muromachi government, Ashikaga Yoshimitsu. It was burnt down in 1467 during the Onin War, but was rebuilt shortly afterward. This temple is the headquarters of the Shokoku-ji School of the Rinzai sect of Zen Buddhism. There are about 100 temples of this school around the country, including the famous Kinkaku-ji Temple, and Ginkaku-ji Temple.

While Nobunaga was active, he stayed in this temple during his visits to Kyoto and he also threw large tea ceremonies from time to time here. Toyotomi Hideyoshi's heir, Hideyori, sponsored the rebuilding of the Hatto (Dharma Hall) in 1605, which is the oldest surviving Hatto in Japan. Its ceiling painting by Kano Mitsunobu, called *Howling Dragon*, is still preserved in its bright colors and is a favorite spot for visitors.

Admission to the temple grounds is free. The special areas, including Hatto, are open during the special admission periods in spring and fall for an admission fee.

Left: *Howling Dragon* at Shokoku-ji; Right: *Sokeizu*, Ito Jakchu, 1759

ODA NOBUNAGA

❷ JOTENKAKU MUSEUM
承天閣美術館

www.shokoku-ji.jp/j_nyukan.html

The Jotenkaku Museum is tucked
away on the grounds of the Shokoku-ji
Temple. It was established as part of
commemoration of the 600-year history
of Shokoku-ji Temple in 1984, and its
collection includes many important
pieces, such as five national treasures
and 143 important cultural properties,
including fine arts from Kinkaku-ji and
Ginkaku-ji temples. You can see such
masterpieces as a bamboo teaspoon
carved by Sen-no-Rikyu, tea bowls by
the famous artist Hon'ami Koetsu, and
other tea utensils, plus famous ink and
Japanese-style paintings created by
Maruyama Okyo, Tawaraya Sohtatsu,
Sesshu, Ikeno Taiga, and others. On
permanent display is *Rokuon-ji Oshoin
Shoheki-ga* (an important cultural
property), a popular ink painting
by the famed Ito Jakuchu, whose
unparalleled technique and uniquely
bold compositions still appeal to visitors.
Exhibition labels and texts are only
in Japanese.

ITO JAKUCHU AND THE PRICE COLLECTION

Joe Price is an American art collector from
California who started collecting Japanese
painting from the Edo period in the 1950s,
at a time when no one else was paying
attention to these art works, not even art
historians. At the center of his collection
are the works of Ito Jakuchu (1716–1800),
a painting genius from the middle Edo
period. Price found Jakuchu's painting for
the first time at an antique art store in New
York, at the time when he was graduating
college. He gravitated to a painting of
grapes and purchased it without knowing
who painted it. He later found out the
artist's name was Ito Jakuchu.

Jakuchu was also a religious man who
had abandoned the secular world for
a life focused on Zen Buddhism. He
studied Zen with the priest at Shokoku-ji,
and the two kept a close relationship.
His talent in painting was in a class by
itself, especially with the outstanding
skills in detailed portrayal and unique
spatial representations.

Although he was well known and popular
at the time he was alive, people had
forgotten about him by the 20th century.
However, thanks to the Price Collection,
Jakuchu's popularity has been soaring
since late 1990s. "Price Collection—
Exhibition of Jakuchu and Edo Paintings"
has circulated among four cities in Japan,
including Tokyo and Kyoto, and has
attracted one million visitors in total since
2006.

KYOTO

WHERE TO SEE

Kinkaku-ji

❸ KINKAKU-JI TEMPLE (TEMPLE OF THE GOLDEN PAVILION)—UNESCO WORLD HERITAGE SITE
金閣寺

Kinkakuji-cho, Kita-ku, Kyoto
075-461-0013

The official name for this temple is Rokuon-ji. One of the Shokoku-ji School temples, it was originally a villa for a high-ranking official in the Kamakura period, its scale as large as that of Kyoto Gosho palace. Ashikaga Yoshimitsu, the third shogun of the Muromachi shogunate, took over and remodeled it in 1397. It became a temple after Yoshimitsu's death. This golden pavilion, a symbol of Kyoto, is actually a *shari-den*, reliquary hall to house the Buddha's remains. The building has three floors;

the second and third floors are gilded, and a shining phoenix sits on top of the roof. The reflection of the golden pavilion on the pond is also beautiful.

The current pavilion was rebuilt in 1952 to restore it to its original condition, which took three years. Another restoration, taking two years from 1986, included the application of special gold leaf, which was five times thicker than normal.

ODA NOBUNAGA

❹ GINKAKU-JI TEMPLE (TEMPLE OF THE SILVER PAVILION)—UNESCO WORLD HERITAGE SITE
銀閣寺

Ginkakuji-cho, Sakyo-ku, Kyoto
075-771-5725

Ginkaku-ji's official name is Jisho-ji and it is also one of the Shokoku-ji School temples. It was originally built by the eighth Muromachi shogun, Ashikaga Yoshimasa, as his mountain villa in Higashi-yama. The wooden structure represents the culmination of beauty in elegant simplicity that Yoshimasa developed through a lifetime of creative pursuits. It is believed that its study/ living room is the origin of the tea ceremony room. Yoshimasa started building the Ginkaku pavilion in 1490, but died before seeing its completion. It was turned into a temple of the Rinzai Sect, in accordance with Yoshimasa's will. It is interesting to see the clear difference in style between Kinkaku-ji, which was built before the Onin War (1467–1477), and Ginkaku-ji, which was built after.

❺ MYOKAKU-JI TEMPLE
妙覚寺

Shin-machi Kashira Kurama-guchi Sagaru, Kamigyo-ku, Kyoto (Kamigoryomae-dori Fukagawa Higashi-iru)
075-441-2802

Myokaku-ji temple was originally established in 1378, but was burned down and moved to Sakai, Osaka. It was reestablished by Nichijo, who was a son of the lord of the Mino region, Saito Dosan. Dosan was the father of Oda Nobunaga's wife, and Nobunaga used this temple to hold luxurious tea ceremonies. At the time of the Incident at Honno-ji, Nobunaga's heir, Oda Nobutada, was staying here. In the year following the death of Nobunaga, Toyotomi Hideyoshi redesigned the capital and ordered the temple to be relocated; it was rebuilt in 1584 at its current location. Its garden is a hidden gem, especially for autumn foliage. Admission is free for the temple grounds (Fee for the main hall and garden. Reservations are preferred.)

Ginkaku-ji

❻ DAITOKU-JI TEMPLE SOKEN-IN
大徳寺・総見院

59 Daitokuji-cho, Murasakino,
Kita-ku, Kyoto
075-492-2630

Soken-in is a temple that Toyotomi Hideyoshi established in 1583 in order to console the spirit of Oda Nobunaga after his death in the Incident at Honno-ji. Soken-in is the posthumous Buddhist name for Nobunaga. Hideyoshi carried out a grand funeral for Nobunaga here. Hideyoshi made two wooden statutes of Nobunaga, one of which was made from the aromatic wood of the agarwood tree and was cremated with the ashes of Honno-ji Temple instead of Nobunaga's actual remains. It is said that the fragrance filled the air of the entire capital city. In 1585, Hideyoshi held a tea ceremony as a memorial to Nobunaga where Hideyoshi personally whisked tea for the guests. There are still three tea ceremony rooms in this temple.

Soken-in is not regularly open to public (Special public viewing periods are held in spring and fall each year. http://icom-kyotosyunjyu.com/english-top/)

Daitoku-ji Temple, where the Soken-in stands, was established in 1315 during the late Kamakura period. Although this temple was devastated in the Onin War, it was rebuilt by the monk Ikkyu. When Hideyoshi established Soken-in, he donated some land for this temple. After this, other warlords followed to build many more sub-temples. The second floor of the temple gate was added by Sen-no-Rikyu where he placed a statute of himself. They say that Hideyoshi was so infuriated by this that he ordered Rikyu to commit *seppuku* (ritual suicide).

Today, Daitoku-ji has 22 sub-temples. Many of them have the graves of warlords and generals, as well as elegant dry landscape gardens. More characteristically, there are 29 tea ceremony rooms within the Daitoku-ji complex.

Kinmo-kaku gate, where Sen-no-Rikyu placed a statute of himself

❼ NIJO CASTLE—UNESCO WORLD HERITAGE SITE
二条城

Nijojo-cho, Nijodori Horikawa Nishi-iru,
Nakagyo-ku, Kyoto
075-841-0096
English brochure: (PDF)
www.city.kyoto.jp/bunshi/nijojo/english1.pdf

Nijo Castle

Nijo Castle was originally established by Nobunaga in 1569 on behalf of the shogun Ashikaga Yoshiaki. Its location was northeast of the current Nijo Castle, near the southern end of Kyoto Gyoen. In 1570, Nobunaga held a tea ceremony at the newly built castle and many lords came from around the country. When Nobunaga expelled Yoshiaki in 1573, he burnt down the castle out of spite. The remains of this old castle were discovered during an excavation survey in 1975, along with remains of the stone walls and the moat.

In 1578, five years after Nobunaga destroyed the castle, he built a glorious new Nijo Castle at a different location (at the corner of Nijo and Muromachi streets) where he would stay when visiting Kyoto. A year later, he gave this castle to Prince Sanehito. It was called Nijo Gosho as opposed to the *Gosho* (Imperial Palace) where the emperor resided. Just three years later, Nobunaga died; Nijo castle was burned down at the same time. Later, Hideyoshi built a new castle at the west of the old location, and also called it Nijo Castle.

Then, who built the current Nijo Castle, which is so popular with tourists? The shogun Tokugawa Ieyasu constructed this new castle as his residence when he was in Kyoto. The current location is to the west of the previous Nijo castles built by Nobunaga and Hideyoshi. It was originally completed in 1603, and the third shogun, Iemitsu, Ieyasu's grandson, added and enlarged structures like the castle's keep. The current structure was finally completed in 1626. In 1867, at the end of Tokugawa shogunate, the fifteenth shogun, Yoshinobu, returned governmental power to Emperor Meiji in this castle. For 400 years, this castle observed the history of Japan. Today, it is an important piece of cultural heritage.

Nijo Castle is an important site for understanding the history of Kyoto. You can enjoy the main Ninomaru-goten building (a national treasure), where the best of Momoyama culture can be seen: the gorgeously painted sliding doors by the Kano-school painters, and the magnificent garden where flowers blossom in every season. In spring, 200 cherry trees in the garden are lit up and are so beautiful. The vast grounds are about the size of six baseball fields. The stone wall of the old Nijo Castle, built by Nobunaga, is restored and displayed at the corner.

KYOTO

安土

AZUCHI

View from the Azuchi Castle site

Visiting the Remains of Nobunaga's Dream, Azuchi Castle

The life of Nobunaga is filled with mysterious legends. Among them, Azuchi Castle, the so-called phantom castle with its many unsolved mysteries. Nobunaga started building Azuchi Castle in 1576 when he had reached the height of his power in the nation. Three years later, in 1579, the grand castle, with Japan's first castle tower, which was unparalleled by any other, was completed. According to some records, it was an innovative castle, suited for Nobunaga, who was a pioneer in every aspect. The castle itself was like a fine work of art, decorated with gold everywhere.

The Portuguese missionary Luís Froís saw this castle and was very surprised at the sight of its magnificent tower, which was 108 feet (33 meters) tall, six floors above ground and one floor underground. As he wrote in his *History of Japan*: "It is comparable to the most superb castles in Europe in terms of the structure, solidity, furnishings, treasures, and gorgeousness. In the center of the castle, there is a kind of a tower that they call *ten-shu*, which is more elegant and grand than our towers in Europe."

However, just three years later, this beautiful castle was burned down right after Nobunaga killed himself at Honno-ji Temple. Both the gorgeous castle tower and palace were turned to ashes, and very few historical materials remaining to describe this castle, shrouding it in mystery. Even today, it is not known who set fire to the castle. Just as Nobunaga abruptly disappeared moments before unifying the country, this castle's fate is so dramatic that people cannot stop wondering about the truth.

Azuchi Castle Museum

JR Azuchi Station is 45 minutes by train from Kyoto. It would make a nice day excursion from Kyoto. You will see a statute of Nobunaga when you step out of the station, but it is quite calm here compared to a typical tourist town.

After leaving the ticket gate at the station, you can take the underground passage to get to the south plaza where the Azuchi Castle Museum is located. It is advisable that you see the one-twentieth-scale replica of Azuchi Castle here on display to get an image of the castle before you go visit its ruins, where little remains but some stone walls.

This replica is made elaborately to detail and designed to reveal the interior of the castle tower. Surprisingly, there is an atrium inside the tower, a feature not seen in traditional Japanese buildings. It is assumed that Nobunaga attempted to copy the European church structures that he heard about from missionaries.

This castle is believed to represent Nobunaga's philosophy and dreams. It is said, "If you understand Azuchi Castle, you understand Nobunaga."

ODA NOBUNAGA

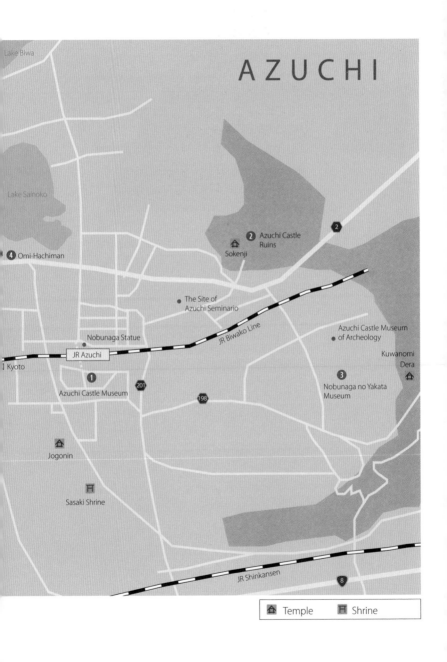

AZUCHI

Lake Biwa

Lake Sainoko

Omi-Hachiman

Azuchi Castle Ruins

Sokenji

The Site of Azuchi Seminario

JR Biwako Line

Nobunaga Statue

JR Azuchi

Kyoto

Azuchi Castle Museum of Archeology

Kuwanomi Dera

Azuchi Castle Museum

Nobunaga no Yakata Museum

201

198

Jogonin

Sasaki Shrine

JR Shinkansen

Temple   Shrine

Azuchi Castle replica at Azuchi Castle Museum

The existence of the castle's tower atrium, which represents Nobunaga's innovative mind, was revealed during a large-scale excavation survey between 1989 and 2008. We are finally beginning to see the entire image of Azuchi Castle and Nobunaga's ideals after 430 years.

Let's visit the ruins of Azuchi Castle with these newly discovered truths in mind.

Visiting the Ruins of Azuchi Castle

Nobunaga was at the height of his power when he built Azuchi Castle, and the castle sent the message that he was the most powerful ruler in Japan. Why did he choose this location? It was close to Kyoto, and also at a key junction of transportation where Nobunaga could pay attention to both the western and eastern sides of the country. Moreover, this land had rich soil and both people and money were drawn here. It was a convenient location for Nobunaga, who was aiming to unite the country by taking advantage of the authority of the imperial court. Three sides of the castle were

ODA NOBUNAGA

NOBUNAGA'S FOLDING SCREEN GOES TO ROME

Oda Nobunaga sent a folding picture screen to Pope Gregory XIII in the Vatican as a gift. It is known as *Azuchiyama-zu-byoubu* (Folding Screen with an Image of Mount Azuchi). Nobunaga had ordered Kano Eitoku to capture the sight of Azuchi Castle and its surrounding city in details. The emperor was stunned by the beauty of the screen and asked for it, but Nobunaga refused and gave it instead to the Jesuit missionary Alessandro Valignano. The screen was then sent to Rome, in the hands of the Tensho boys' embassy. Nobunaga must have wanted Europe to see the magnificence of Azuchi Castle.

The Tensho embassy consisted of four young men who were studying Christianity at a *seminario* in Arima (Nagasaki Prefecture). They left for Rome with the folding screen four months before the Incident at Honno-ji. The embassy took three years to reach Rome via Goa, Lisbon, and other cities, before finally having an audience with Pope Gregory XIII. The records show that the Pope was impressed with this beautiful artwork and had it placed in the Corridor of Maps in the Vatican. Unfortunately, however, the Pope died shortly after their visit and the folding screen has been missing for 400 years. A survey confirmed that the folding screen was still in the Corridor of Maps in 1592, but its further whereabouts have been unknown.

There are some different theories regarding the appearance and structure of Azuchi Castle. If the folding screen is ever found, we would be able to learn the full picture of the castle and also solve the many mysteries about Azuchi Castle and Nobunaga. In recent years, Shiga Prefecture and Azuchi City (where Azuchi Castle was located) have been sending survey groups to Rome to investigate the whereabouts of the folding screen. There have even been efforts to look for the screen by means of social networks. Hopefully, the Mount Azuchi Picture Screen will be discovered and offer answers to these mysteries in the near future.

Images of Azuchi Castle and the Tensho embassy from the Azuchi Castle Museum

The Ote-michi stairs at Azuchi Castle

surrounded by the water of Lake Biwa, the largest lake in Japan, and easy to defend from enemies; he could also get to Kyoto in a swift manner via boat.

But land reclamation projects around the lake have progressed, and this location is now surrounded by land in all directions. Today, all you see around Azuchi Mountain is a vast rustic land. There is no remnant of the once-busy castle town where the vassals' mansions were standing shoulder to shoulder and merchants from all over the country came to do business.

You can walk to the castle ruin from the station in 25 minutes. However, if you want to save time and energy, you can ride in a taxi or rent a bike at the station.

At the entrance to the castle, the long stone stairs, Ote-michi, which are 20 feet (6 meters) wide, stretch straight up as if reaching to the sky. Once, the sky-spearing castle tower must have stood tall above these stone stairs. It is known that the castle tower was built to be especially beautiful on the south side, which was facing the main street.

In other words, this street to the castle was built to show off the greatness of the castle and of Nobunaga's power. (Though his vassals and the like took other routes to

ODA NOBUNAGA

the castle from the town.) It explains why he laid out a straight street to the castle, which defied military common sense. The castle was his residence as well as a defensive stronghold.

The stone stairs of the main street have been recently restored to their original state, by excavating what was buried under the soil for 400 years. When you actually try to walk up this stairs, you will find how tricky it is. The slope is fairly steep where even the small steps are about 12 inches (30 cm) high and tall steps are about 20 inches (50 cm) high; they are set randomly to make it very difficult to walk up. It appears to be a simple straight street, but it is actually carefully designed to be hard to climb.

Along the side of the stone stairs lie the ruins of the residences of Hideyoshi and other vassals. The cornerstones of these buildings were discovered and signs were placed with explanations. After a while, the street starts to wind its way up in a zigzag. It cannot be very easy to climb, even on a horse, as Nobunaga cleverly planned. After a heart-pounding walk of 30 to 40 minutes, you can finally get to the top where the castle tower used to stand.

Cornerstones mark the sites of the palace and castle tower. From the

WHAT IS SEMINARIO?

Seminarios were the facilities for Christian religious education set up by the Jesuits to train Japanese clergymen. Valignano opened such schools in Arima and Azuchi in 1580 and taught Christian doctrine, as well as Latin, Western music, arts and crafts, and so on. However, after the Incident at Honno-ji in 1582, the seminario in Azuchi lost its support and had to move to Kyoto, Osaka, and other places until it merged with the seminario in Nagasaki in 1588. In 1613, the Tokugawa government issued the Anti-Christian Edicts and the seminario closed the following year.

THE TRAGEDY OF THE TENSHO EMBASSY

In 1582, when the Jesuit missionary Alessandro Valignano left Japan, Nobunaga made a plan to send a Japanese envoy to the Pope, bringing with them the Mount Azuchi Picture Screen. He selected four young men of ages between 12 and 14 years old from the Christian *daimyos* (feudal lords) in the Kyushu region. The embassy passed Goa, Lisbon, Madrid, and Florence to reach Rome, and finally had an audience with the Pope.

Though they received enthusiastic receptions everywhere they visited, by the time they returned to Japan in 1590, Christianity had been banned by Toyotomi Hideyoshi. The anti-Christian enforcement became more strict by the year, and the young men of the Tensho embassy either had to abandon their faith, be exiled, or face execution. Although these emissaries had to follow such a tragic destiny, they left enormous achievements: they brought back printing press machines and printing techniques, and appealed for Japan to the Christian world.

Azuchi Castle tower site

excavation survey, it was discovered that Nobunaga had built a building for inviting the emperor to his palace, further confirming that Nobunaga was trying to take advantage of the emperor's authority. Interestingly, Hideyoshi later remodeled the Seiryoden (the emperor's residence) at Kyoto Gosho by almost exactly duplicating this palace in Azuchi Castle (only east and west were reversed). In turn, the Tokugawa shogunate followed this example. Thus, the original form of the current Seiryoden at Kyoto Gosho was actually created by Nobunaga.

Nobunaga's Dream Castle Tower

The castle tower was standing on a peak, which is a little higher than the palace site. The tower was Japan's first tall building, with a total of seven floors—one floor underground and six floors above—and it was 131 feet (40 meters) wide in the south-north direction and 112 feet (34 meters) wide from east to west. And all this was standing on the top of Azuchi Mountain, which is 653 feet (199 meters) tall. It must have been an astounding sight for the people of the time.

ODA NOBUNAGA

Castles were originally built as military forts. Azuchi Castle was the first one in Japanese history to have a real tower structure. Against the common practice of the time, Nobunaga regularly resided in the tower while all other lords resided in their palaces. At a time when buildings were all single-storied in Japan, people could not conceive of living on the second floor or above.

The missionary Luís Fróis described the details of the castle tower in his book *History of Japan* as follows: "All four walls of the interior are filled with paintings of images in gold and other bright colors. The exterior was painted in a different color according to the floor." As Frois described, the exterior of the top floor was gold and other floors were painted separately in red, white, blue, and other colors. Inside the castle, each room was decorated with paintings of the era's top painter, Kano Eitoku.

After Nobunaga passed away, Hideyoshi and Ieyasu built castle towers taller than that of Azuchi Castle. However, they merely competed on the height of the towers and did not have their own design philosophies. Also, the function of those towers was only to decorate the castles or to offer shelter in case of emergencies.

Then, what part of Nobunaga's philosophy was built into this castle?

First, it is believed that Nobunaga placed a Buddhist *stupa* (a mound that holds religious relics, intended as a place of worship) in the bottom of the atrium of the tower. It was rare that such a religious article was found in a castle, which was an instrument of wars. Furthermore, this castle seems to have been a religious facility with the elements not only of Buddhism, but also of Confucianism, Shintoism, and Christianity.

Life-size replica of the top part of the Azuchi Castle tower at Nobunaga no Yakata

ODA NOBUNAGA

For example, the sixth level from the bottom (the fifth floor) was in an octagon shape and the interior was structured as a spiral. The exterior was painted with scenes of hell and the interior was all golden with painted images of Buddha and his ten disciples. It seems to imply that the world of endless war would become as peaceful as the Buddhist pure land once Nobunaga unified it.

The top floor was in a square shape and painted with images using the themes from ancient Chinese philosophies, such as images of Lao Tzu and Confucius. This floor is believed to present Nobunaga's political ideals after he achieved peace in the land. Nobunaga must have spent some time alone pondering in this room.

In short, this castle tower was not merely a decorative structure of the castle, but a residence, as well as a space for ceremonies (there was a stage hanging in the atrium on the third level from the bottom), a religious symbol, and a space for philosophical contemplation. Nobunaga is often associated with an image of a cold-hearted outrageous tyrant, who feared neither gods nor Buddhas. However, based on the results from the most recent research of Azuchi Castle, a whole different picture of Nobunaga appears.

Nonetheless, Azuchi Castle, which expressed Nobunaga's philosophy in stone, disappeared with all its valuable fine art, including Kano Eitoku's paintings, and his intentions have not been known fully in history. Scholars say that the excavation survey was as if they were challenging wits with Nobunaga. The survey is still in progress. Depending on the results, it is still possible to change people's image of Nobunaga and Japanese history.

At the ruins of the castle tower on the mountain peak, all you can see are the cornerstones neatly lined up. However, feeling the breeze from Lake Biwa, you could give a thought to what Nobunaga aimed for or dreamed of. When you spend a little time imagining the castle that disappeared as though a dream on this open spot, you can feel a personal closeness with Nobunaga.

At the foot of the castle tower's ruins, there are the ruins of Ni-no-maru (the second palace). Nobunaga's tomb is standing here, but what is buried here is only a memento, just like the other tombs in Kyoto.

Soken-ji Temple

On the way down from the peak, you can take a different route, which leads to the old site of Nobunaga's family temple, Soken-ji. Nobunaga transferred this temple to this mountainside spot from another location when he built Azuchi Castle. It survived after the castle fell, and you can see a quaint three-layer tower (established in 1454 and transferred to this location when the castle was built), and the Nio-mon Gate (built in 1571 and transferred here as well) in their original condition. (The temple's main hall building burned down in the 19th century and a temporary building has been built along the side of the Ote-michi.)

Soken, as in the name of Soken-ji Temple, means "to gather all religions and philosophies of the world." Nobunaga's thoughts are evident in the name. There is an overlook at the ruins of the temple main hall and gives you a great view of Azuchi. Nobunaga must have liked this view and chose this site for the temple.

It is actually an interesting idea that Nobunaga built a temple within the castle. Moreover, he built a route to the castle going through these temple grounds. Many

The Three-Layer Tower at the Soken-ji Temple

of those who went to Azuchi Castle at the time took this route rather than the main street, Ote-michi. It is impressive to discover that as they climbed up this route to the castle, they could look up the gorgeous castle tower over the Nio-mon temple gate. It must have been breathtakingly beautiful for those who visited Azuchi Castle for the first time. As a superb creative director, Nobunaga must have designed this as part of the castle, calculating every effect to show off.

The castle complex had stone walls everywhere and gathering enough raw material was not an easy task. Large stones were needed to build these walls and had to carry up to the mountaintop. A gigantic rock called *Ja-ishi* (serpent's stone) took about 10,000 laborers to get it up the mountain. According to Fróis's *History of Japan*, as they were pulling this stone up the mountain, an accident happened and over 150 people were crushed. Everything about this project was large in scale.

Unfortunately, there is no plan to rebuild this impressive castle as a whole.

WHERE TO SEE

Nobunaga statue at Azuchi Station

❶ AZUCHI CASTLE MUSEUM
安土城郭資料館

700 Konaka, Azuchi-cho, Omihachiman
0748-46-5616

The Azuchi Castle Museum is located at the south plaza of JR Azuchi Station. The exhibits include the very detailed one-twentieth-scale replica of Azuchi Castle, ceramic wall art in a folding screen style depicting the Tensho boys' embassy's journey to Rome, and replicas of the interior paintings of Azuchi Castle. A café is located inside. A *sumo-yagura* (a tower for sumo performance) is at the neighboring site.

❷ AZUCHI CASTLE RUINS
安土城址

Shimotoira, Azuchi-cho, Omihachiman
0748-46-2142

These are the ruins of the castle Nobunaga built on Mt. Azuchi. Even though the castle buildings do not exist anymore, the original stone steps of Ote-michi were recently restored, and there are enough places of interest. On the hillside, Soken-ji Temple's three-layer tower and the Nio-mon Gate (both originally built between the 15th century to 16th century and transferred here) are standing the way they were when Azuchi Castle was built under Nobunaga. It takes about an hour to an hour and a half to look around. It requires some physical strength to climb up the steep stone stairs, but the scenery from the mountaintop and the observatory near the three-level tower are indescribable. Near the entrance, there is the provisional main building of Soken-ji, on the old site of Ieyasu Tokugawa's residence. You can look inside for a fee. Every June, there is the Azuchi Nobunaga Festival, where a procession of costumed warriors marches from the train station to the castle ruins.

ODA NOBUNAGA

❸ NOBUNAGA NO YAKATA (HOUSE OF NOBUNAGA) MUSEUM
信長の館

800 Kuwanomi-ji, Azuchi-cho, Omihachiman
0748-46-6512

You can see the life-size replica of the top part of Azuchi Castle tower in this museum. This replica was created as the main exhibition of the Japanese pavilion for the Universal Exposition of Seville in 1992. After the Expo ended, it was given to Azuchi City where it is displayed to the public. The replica, relied on the most trusted theory about the structure of Azuchi Castle, is a sophisticated reproduction of the interior of the tower, which is decorated with the golden paintings by Kano Eitoku. The model includes the golden exterior of the sixth floor, made from 100,000 pieces of gold leaf, as well as the great roof with the golden *shachihoko* (decoration in the shape of a fish-like creature with the head of a tiger). In addition, a replica of the banquet menu that Nobunaga offered to Tokugawa Ieyasu in May of 1582 is on display.

❹ OMIHACHIMAN
近江八幡

Three years after Nobunaga's death, Toyotomi Hidetsugu, who was going to succeed Hideyoshi, established Hachiman-yama Castle in Omihachiman near Azuchi. He ordered the residents of the town surrounding Azuchi Castle to move to Omihachiman. While the town of Azuchi became desolate, the town surrounding Hachiman-yama Castle became prosperous as a leading commercial town under the policy of *Rakuichi Rakuza* (free markets and open guilds).

Even today, tourists visit the historic streets where the prosperous Omi merchants' mansions still stand. The area along the Hachiman-bori canal has an especially attractive atmosphere, ideal for taking a walk. Omihachiman is just a station away from Azuchi by JR. Since there are so few restaurants in Azuchi, you may want to stop by at Omihachiman for a meal. There are restaurants that serve high-quality Omi

The Shinmachi of Omihachiman

ODA NOBUNAGA

Former post office building designed by Wiliam Vories

WILLIAM MERREL VORIES AND OMIHACHIMAN

beef. You may want to stop by a very popular Japanese restaurant Himure-chaya, owned by a famous manufacturer of Japanese sweets, who renovated an old folk house, and it is always busy with tourists.

Within the well-preserved historic streets, there are some tasteful Western-style buildings in Omihachiman. The architect who built these buildings was an American by the name of William Merrel Vories. He was also an active businessman and Christian missionary. Born in Kansas, he graduated from Colorado University and became a missionary. He came to Japan at the age of 24 in 1905 and became an English teacher at a local high school. Three years later, he started an architecture business and worked on as many as 1,600 buildings while preaching the Gospel. He established a company to import and sell Mentholatum ointment in Japan (today's Omi Corp.); he also built a sanatorium for treating tuberculosis (today's Vories Memorial Hospital) and schools, while actively contributed to the local society. Vories's dedication to and passion for Omihachiman is still visible in this city today.

Statue of William Merrel Vories

坂本龍馬
SAKAMOTO RYOMA

Portrait of Sakamoto Ryoma, 1866-67

Sakamoto Ryoma, the Hero of the Meiji Restoration, and Fushimi

The Tokugawa shogunate fell in the middle of the 19th century, ending the era of the samurai, and making way for the modernization of Japan. One young man was instrumental in this reform. His name was Sakamoto Ryoma.

He wrote to his older sister, in his hometown, that he planned to "clean up Japan once and for all."

Ryoma was worried that Japan was going to become prey to the Western powers if things remained the same. He felt the need to overthrow the Tokugawa shogunate, and reunite Japan under the emperor.

Ryoma was known to be a good correspondent. Like the old saying, "Writing and nature often agree," Ryoma's letters and handwriting show his personal charm. His sense of humor is evident when he wrote "launder" when referring to his plans to reform Japan.

Landing at Yokohama, William Heine, 1854

Although he was just a *dappan ronin,* a masterless
samurai who had left his fief without permission, he
dedicated himself to successfully organizing a coalition
between the Satsuma (now Kagoshima prefecture)
and the Choshu (now Yamaguchi prefecture) clans to
form a powerful opposition against the Edo shogunate,
overthrowing it. The fact that the Edo shogunate
returned power to the emperor in a peaceful manner
owed much to his efforts.

Ryoma wrote "The Eight Point Program," for the
modernization of Japan. Calling for a restoration of the
emperor, and laying out ideas for government, military
and trade, it became the basic political guideline for the
new government and cabinet after the Meiji Restoration.
He also established Kameyama Shachu (later, Kaien-tai),
a precursor of early import/export companies. In
Nagasaki, he did business with the Scottish trading
merchant Thomas Blake Glover and showed interests in
further activities overseas.

Ryoma longed for a society that was free and equal
without class distinctions, like the Western countries
at the time. He dreamed of traveling to the United

States and England once his big job leading "Japan's resurrection" was achieved. In spite of his dream, he was assassinated in Kyoto just a month after the restoration of imperial rule. It was his 33rd birthday. He finished his short life without seeing the birth of the Meiji government.

Having earned many devout followers, Ryoma's life has been novelized and dramatized repeatedly. He is the leading hero of the end of the Edo era. In 2003, he became the first person whose name was used for an airport in Japan. The airport of his hometown, Kochi, is called Kochi Ryoma Airport.

Wearing rare-at-the-time leather boots, and going on the first known honeymoon in Japan, Ryoma had no shortage of memorable episodes. He was an active man with a charming, captivating personality, yet he is not well known outside Japan.

It is said that Romulus Hillsborough, the American who spent seven years researching and writing Ryoma's 1999 biography *Ryoma: Life of a Renaissance Samurai*, was chagrined that so few non-Japanese know of Ryoma.

In his book published in Japan, *Eigo de Yomu Sakamoto Ryoma* (Reading Sakamoto Ryoma in English), Hillsborough wrote the following as the preface:

"So I set about condensing Ryoma's very complicated life into these two small volumes—no easy task. I have focused on the driving forces behind Ryoma's powerful personality: courage, mental toughness, a Herculean perseverance, determination to create a better world—and, perhaps most important of all, a longing for freedom. I believe that these qualities enabled him to bring about his greatest achievement—a peaceful revolution to usher in the modern age."

LIFE OF SANKAMOTO RYOMA

Sakamoto Ryoma can be considered the person who triggered the overthrow of the Tokugawa shogunate. The shogunate government at the time was forced to bow down to demands from other countries and, at the same time, could not enforce its rule over other Japanese clans either. Ryoma acted as go-between for those who believed that the destabilized shogunate could not protect Japan, and the necessity to overthrow the shogunate and reunite the country under the emperor. This became the movement toward the Meiji Restoration.

Sakamoto Ryoma was born on November 15, Tenpo 6 (January 3, 1836), the second eldest son of the Sakamoto family, which were low-ranking samurai. The Sakamoto family was originally a merchant family and Ryoma grew up in the free and logical merchant culture, which appeared to have a great impact on his life.

At the age of 19, he moved to Edo (today's Tokyo) for the study of swordsmanship, and joined one of the three major schools in Edo, the Hokushin Ittoryu Chiba school. In the same year, Commodore Perry's four Black Ships arrived at Uraga, and Ryoma was deployed as part of a coastal guard in Shinagawa. At this time, he wrote to his father, "If a war breaks out, I will decapitate the foreigners and go home to Tosa."

However, when he returned to his hometown a year and a half later, Kawada Shoryo, who was a painter familiar with circumstances in the West, taught him that in order to act equally with the world, Japan would need large ships and the human resources to sail them. Ryoma realized for the first time the situation that Japan was in at the time, and this broadened his view of the world.

He went back to Edo and further practiced swordsmanship, but he became troubled deeper each day that Japan could not be protected by the sword alone. When he was 28 years old, he finally left the Tosa clan. (Fleeing from one's clan meant moving out of the clan's territory without permission; it was a serious crime punishable by the forfeiture of the family name or other severe penalties. However, some clans were already ignoring this kind of conduct by Ryoma's time.)
He then became an apprentice of

The site of Omiya Inn, where Ryoma was assassinated in 1867

Katsu Kaishu, the government's Naval Magistrate, and worked with him while devoted himself to mastering navigation skills at the Kobe Naval Training Center.

Such smooth times were over shortly, when the Naval Training Center and Katsu's school were closed in 1865. Ryoma and other *ronin* (masterless samurai) who had fled from their own clans had nowhere to go. Ryoma received support from the Satsuma clan and established a political organization, as well as an import/export company called Kameyama Shachu in Nagasaki. He purchased warships and guns on behalf of the Satsuma and Choshu clans. In the meantime, he mediated the hostile relationship between the Satsuma and the Choshu, and worked toward a coalition of these two major clans. He also masterminded the movement toward reuniting the country under the emperor's leadership, and this eventually led the Tokugawa shogunate to give up power.

However, Ryoma lost his life before witnessing the birth of the new Meiji government. On November 15, Keio 3 (November 15, 1867), just a month after the Shogunate turned over power to the Emperor, someone assassinated Ryoma while he was at the Omiya Inn in Kyoto. He was only 33 years old.

The major theory of his assassination believes that the shogunate government's *Mimawarigumi* (paramilitary patrol team) was responsible for the assassination. However, there are still other theories for the possible behind-the-scenes suspects that include the Meiji government itself, the Satsuma clan, the Tosa clan, or the Kishu clan. The truth is still a mystery.

WHAT IS A SHOGUN? WHAT IS A SHOGUNATE?

From the 12th to the 19th centuries, the real rulers of Japan were shoguns, military dictators who inherited the post but were nonetheless "appointed" by the emperor. The first shogunate *bakufu*, or administration, was established by Minamoto no Yoritomo in the city of Kamakura; subsequent shogunates included the Ashikaga and Tokugawa. During the Tokugawa shogunate, the shogunate's seat was in Edo. For 250 years during the Edo period, Japan enjoyed relative peace under the shoguns.

Hopefully, more and more people will find out that 150 years ago, while Japan had its doors closed to the outside world, there was an interesting man called Sakamoto Ryoma. He was not a nobleman or someone important in the government, but just a low-ranking samurai from countryside. Nonetheless, he had a vision of the world in a global perspective, and led the revolution of Japan with his passion and humanity.

Ryoma is associated with many places throughout Japan: Kochi, where he was born; Kobe, where he studied sailing at the Naval Training Center; Nagasaki, where he established the Kameyama Shachu trading company; and lastly, Kyoto, where he was assassinated.

In Fushimi, Kyoto, Ryoma left many footsteps behind at places like an inn called Teradaya that he patronized. Let's visit the places associated with Ryoma around this area.

The Horikawa River in Fushimi

SAKAMOTO RYOMA

Ryoma in Fushimi

The main train station for sightseeing the Fushimi area is Chushojima Station, which is 13 minutes away from Sanjo Station in the center of Kyoto on an express train on the Keihan Line. Fushimi is a port town in Kyoto. After the death of Oda Nobunaga, Toyotomi Hideyoshi united the country and built his castle in Fushimi. It is said that Hideyoshi constructed the port here in order to bring the necessary materials to build his castle. Afterwards, Fushimi became prosperous as a castle town, and during the Edo period, it became a river transportation hub connecting Kyoto, Osaka, and other parts of Japan.

Fushimi is also known for its spring water, and there are many sake breweries that take advantage of this tasty water. The Horikawa River used to be the outer moat of Fushimi Castle, along which many quaint-looking sake breweries stand side by side. Some of the breweries welcome tourists to come inside and taste their sake. Do not miss this spot if you are a sake lover.

Fushimi's cherry trees are beautiful in spring and are lit up romantically at night. Edo-era riverboats (Jyukkoku-bune and Sanjyukkoku-bune) have been rebuilt for tourists and relaxing

RYOMA'S PERSONALITY

"People may say whatever. Only I know what I do."

This Japanese-style *tanka* poem is believed to have been written by Ryoma when he was a teenager. It is interpreted to mean that he did not care about how others would view him because it was sufficient for him that he knew what he intended to do. It demonstrates Ryoma's dedication to pursuing his own beliefs at any cost.

Without such a strong beliefs and bold action, it may not have been possible to form an alliance between the Satsuma and Choshu clans and lead the way to the shogun's surrender of his rule to the emperor. Although Ryoma relied on his belief of originality ("Don't mimic others if you want to make things happen," he said) he was open to different opinions from different standpoints and learned the merits of every person. Such flexible thinking and broad connections helped him succeed.

Saigo Takamori was a major figure in the Satsuma clan who lead to the Meiji Restoration together with Ryoma. Saigo said to others, "I've never seen a man with such a big capacity as Ryoma yet." Ryoma had a clear vision of the new era, but he also was a skilled and patient diplomat, with a kind humanity that moved hearts of people.

boat trips run along the river. As these Edo-era boats move slowly in the river under the swaying willow trees, the atmosphere is much more peaceful than in the center of Kyoto.

This river had much busier traffic—travelers taking boats and merchants shipping their goods—when Ryoma was active in this town.

Ancient travelers from Osaka arriving at Fushimi on the Sanjukkoku-bune would walk on the *kaido* (main streets) to go to the center of Kyoto. And there were many inns for those travelers along the way. Teradaya Inn was one of the five largest of these inns and Ryoma was a regular customer.

The landlady of the Teradaya Inn at the time was called Otose, and she was known as a very compassionate woman. She would raise abandoned children and take care of lodgers who had no money. She supported Ryoma and other reform activists; Ryoma affectionately called her Mom.

Teradaya Inn entered the historical record because it was raided while Ryoma was staying here. Late on the night of January 23, Keio 2 (March 9, 1866), Ryoma was resting at Teradaya when Fushimi government officers made a raid. A young girl named Oryo who worked at the inn sensed that the officials were surrounding when she was taking a bath. She quickly went upstairs to inform Ryoma of the danger. Ryoma used a gun and his bodyguard Miyoshi Shinzo used his spear to fight the officers rushing in with spears in their hands. Ryoma was injured but managed to escape into the Satsuma clan mansion.

The Teradaya Incident is the one of the most popular scenes among the dramas and novels that portray Ryoma's life. The highlight of the tale is when Oryo

SAKAMOTO RYOMA

A painting of the Incident at Teradaya; a photograph of Oryo

rushes out of the bathtub to Ryoma's room, nearly naked. Ryoma survived thanks to her wits and he and Oryo married soon afterward. (Some believe that they were already wed before this incident.) The newlyweds traveled together to Kagoshima while Ryoma healed his wounds. People started calling this trip Japan's first honeymoon. At that time, their intimate travel was likely looked down upon by many. It took another fifty years before honeymooning became customary in Japan.

The Teradaya Inn building burned down two years after this incident, but it was rebuilt and is still operating as an inn today. It maintains the old-fashioned appearance, attracting tourists as a historic site associated with Ryoma.

You will see a large Japanese lantern with the name of the inn at the gate. Inside the entrance, there are photos of Ryoma and Otose on the walls. Ryoma's bronze statute stands inside the courtyard. There is a room called "Ume-no-ma" (plum room) on the second floor, where Ryoma stayed. You can see a sword cut supposedly made during the raid incident, an old-fashioned bath, and the back stairway that Oryo used to run upstairs. However, the real building was burned down and no longer exists.

JOHN MANJIRO AND KAWADA SHORYO

The artist Kawada Shoryo is known to have shown young Ryoma a global point of view. But how did Kawada have such knowledge? Kawada had learned about the living and social conditions of the West from John Manjiro (Nakahama Manjiro, or John Mung as he was nicknamed in the United States), who had lived in the U.S. for ten years, at a time when leaving Japan was punishable by death.

John Manjiro

with him at his home and taught Manjiro how to read and write Japanese while he questioned Manjiro about his life abroad. Kawada was surprised to learn from Manjiro how advanced the U.S. was compared to Japan.

Manjiro was a fisherman from Tosa. When he was 14 years old, his ship was wrecked in a storm and was rescued by an American whaling vessel. He was taken to Fairhaven, Massachusetts, and adopted by Captain William Whitfield. There he studied navigation, surveying, and shipbuilding. It is said that Manjiro was so Americanized that he could hardly speak any Japanese by the time he returned to Japan after ten years. Kawada, who was acquainted with the Dutch language, let Manjiro stay

Manjiro was one of the first Japanese who had landed in the U.S., and who became a key person to initiate communications between Japan and the U.S. The knowledge and skills that Manjiro brought home from the U.S. had a great influence on Japan during its transitional period from the end of the Edo period to the Meiji era.

In the United States, Manjiro's story lives on in the picture book *Manjiro: The Boy Who Risked His Life for Two Countries* by Emily Arnold McCully, as well as biographies for children, such as *Shipwrecked!: The True Adventures of a Japanese Boy* by Rhoda Blumberg and *Heart of a Samurai* by Margi Preus.

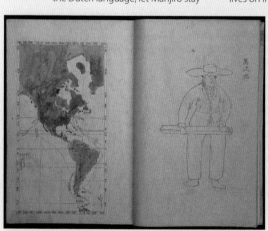

Hyoson Kiryaku (Records of the Drifters), edited by Kawada Shoryo, 1852. The person on the right page is John Manjiro.

SAKAMOTO RYOMA

Teradaya Inn

There is some criticism that it is a betrayal to history to display a replica as if it is the real thing.

Nonetheless, visitors do not seem to care very much whether it is replica or not. They come to this inn to enjoy the realistic historical atmosphere and to feel closer to Ryoma himself.

If you are interested in having a first-hand experience of the atmosphere inside a travelers' inn from the end of Edo period, you can stay overnight in this old inn for a reasonable price of 6,500 yen per night for an adult (not including meals). Ryoma's Ume-no-ma is not available for accommodation.

You can have meals in the surrounding restaurants, which are remodeled sake breweries. Richly-textured fresh zaru tofu and locally manufactured sake made with Fushimi's excellent water are recommended. Also, it is fun to look for Ryoma character items in the Ryoma-dori shopping street right near the inn.

RYOMA AND HIS LETTERS

Ryoma is known as a person of letters. He wrote a large number of letters in his short life of 33 years. More than 130 of his letters have been confirmed and are housed in Kyoto National Museum and in others.

He wrote about his grand plan for the new nation, as well as heartwarming private letters to his sisters and nieces in his hometown, to his first love and to the landlady of the Teradaya Inn, Otose, and to others. Through these letters, we can learn about aspects of his personality, such as his persuasiveness and his scrupulous attention to the people around him and so on.

He wrote about the details of the incident at the Teradaya Inn, where he narrowly escaped assassins, and also how he and his wife Oryo climbed Mt. Kirishima on their honeymoon to Kagoshima. His letters are very charming—he wrote with wit and sometimes included illustrations.

Ryoma's letter describing his climb up Mt. Kirishima on his honeymoon, addressed to his older sister Otome.

Why did Ryoma become the target of the raid by officers? He had just succeeded in forming an alliance between the Satsuma and the Choshu clan a day before, acting as go-between.

In order to overthrow the shogunate and create a modern nation, powerful clans such as Satsuma and Choshu could not be confrontational to each other. They needed to unite their power for the sake of all of Japan. Ryoma believed so and urged the two largest clans to work together to create a large enough force to oppose the shogunate.

Uniting the Satsuma and Choshu was a huge threat for the Edo shogunate. Ryoma, the key player behind this movement, became the target of a manhunt.

Even though the risk to his life was intensifying day by day, Ryoma passionately kept working for the cause. While the Satsuma and Choshu were considering overthrowing the shogunate by force, the Tosa clan was looking to avoid such a conflict. Seeking a peaceful solution, Ryoma proposed eight rules to the Tosa clan, including the shogunate's return of ruling power to the emperor. Because he wrote these rules while he was traveling on a ship to Kyoto from Nagasaki, people later called the plan

SAKAMOTO RYOMA

The Great Stateroom at Nijo Castle

Senchu Hassaku (The Eight Point Program Composed on a Ship). This program became the basic outline for the new government.

The Tosa clan was impressed with Ryoma's idea and advised the fifteenth shogun, Tokugawa Yoshinobu, to return ruling power to the emperor. Accepting this advice, Yoshinobu returned power to Emperor Meiji on October 14, Keio 3 (November 9, 1867).

The historic ceremony took place in Nijo Castle in Kyoto. Yoshinobu gathered the chief vassals from all the clans in the great stateroom in the Ninomaru palace of Nijo Castle and announced the restoration of imperial rule.

Today, in Nijo Castle, life-size figures recreate the scene in the great stateroom, which is included as part of the visitors' tour. This great stateroom is the surviving witness of an important event in history. Japan may not have become what it is today without Ryoma—knowing of Ryoma's critical role behind this historic scene should make your visit to Nijo Castle much more interesting.

Statues of Ryoma and Nakaoka Shintaro in Maruyama Park and Ryozen Museum of History

Unfortunately, however, this hero of the revolution departed this world without seeing the dawn of the new nation.

Just a month after the political revolution, on the evening of November 15, Keio 3 (December 10 1867), Ryoma was assassinated along with his fellow activist, Nakaoka Shintaro, while they were hiding in a guest room of the Omiya Inn in Kawaramachi, Kyoto.

It is believed that Ryoma was attacked by several assassins and received a fatal wound by just a single swing of a sword. However, it is not clear how he was killed so easily in spite of being a great swordsman himself, or who actually ordered the men to kill him. Though there are many mysteries regarding the death of Ryoma even today, one thing for sure was that he was looked upon as an enemy by a multiple factions of the time.

Ryoma's final place on earth, Omiya Inn, no longer exists, and there is only a monument marking "The Place of Distress of Sakamoto Ryoma and Nakaoka Shintaro." But

SAKAMOTO RYOMA

it goes rather unnoticed, standing in the middle of the crowded street of Kawaramachi-dori.

The folding screen and hanging scroll spattered with Ryoma's blood from his assassination are registered as Important Cultural Properties and are housed in the Kyoto National Museum.

You can walk from the location of Ryoma's assassination along the Shijo-dori toward Higashiyama where you will find many popular sightseeing spots, including Yasaka Shrine, Maruyama Park, the Chion-in Temple, and Kiyomizu-dera Temple. This is a popular tourist area and a must-see if you are in Kyoto for the first time.

As a matter of fact, you can find quite a few places related to Ryoma in this neighborhood. In Maruyama Park, famous for its cherry trees, there is a statute of Ryoma and Nakaoka Shintaro. Although there are a number of statutes of Ryoma around the country, this one is special, featuring Ryoma and Nakaoka standing together, and it is very popular among Ryoma fans.

South of the Kodai-ji Temple, there is a path called Ishin-no-michi (street of the restoration) that is the approach to the Kyoto Ryozen Gokoku Shrine, where a number of fallen activists who died just before the Meiji Restoration, including Ryoma and Nakaoka Shintaro, rest. Facing the shrine is the Ryozen Museum of History, which exhibits Ryoma's letters and other historic materials relating to the Meiji Restoration—this entire area is a kind of sacred place for fans of Ryoma.

Right now, Japan is facing rapid changes equivalent to those of the Meiji Restoration. Many Japanese are wondering what Ryoma would think if he were alive today.

WHERE TO SEE

❶ TERADAYA INN
寺田屋

Teradaya Inn
263 Minamihama-cho, Fushimi, Kyoto
075-622-0243 (for sightseeing)
075-622-0252 (for room reservation)

The Teradaya Inn was a traveler's inn that Ryoma stayed at regularly, and where he was attacked by officers of the Fushimi magistrate's office. Today, the inn has a replica of the room where Ryoma was attacked. It is a must-see spot for tourists visiting Ryoma-related sites. Teradaya is still operating as an inn, and you can stay overnight in this historic place.

The Terada-ya Inn opened in 1592 for travelers when Fushimi started attracting people and trade. At the time, there was a wharf called Teradaya-hama, a beach right in front of the inn and many people were passing through. Ryoma had an attachment to the inn's landlady, Otose, who was running a successful business by herself after her debauched husband had passed away. Her tomb

Ume-no-ma room, where Ryoma stayed on the night of the Teradaya Incident

SAKAMOTO RYOMA

is in the cemetery of Shorin-in Temple near the inn.

❷ JYUKKOKU-BUNE BOAT
十石船

075-623-1030
Boarding locations:
JYUKKOKU-BUNE BOATS
behind Gekkeikan Okura

SANJYUKKOKU-BUNE BOATS
Teradayahama Beach

Jyukkoku-bune boats on the Horikawa River

After Toyotomi Hideyoshi reconstructed the Uji River and improved Fushimi's port, this port became a major connection between Osaka and Kyoto, which made the town very prosperous, attracting daily commodities including rice, sake, and lumber, and also many people. Fushimi's water transportation industry became even more prosperous during the Edo period, attracting thousands of boats, until land transportation such as railroads became the mainstream.

Those boats, which were active in Edo period, are now remodeled as tourist boats and operate along the Horikawa River, which was originally the outer moat of Fushimi Castle. The sightseeing course, which runs smoothly by some sake breweries and Teradaya Inn, is relaxing and nostalgic. Imagine Ryoma riding in boats like this as you enjoy the breeze from the river. When the cherry blossoms are lit up at night during the spring, the Jyukkoku-bune boats sail past this fantastic evening scenery.

Boats run April to late November.
Closed during winter.
Duration of trip: approximately 55 minutes (round trip)
The capacity of Jyukkoku-bune boats is 15 people. During the weekends and holidays, Sanjyukkoku-bune boats (30 people capacity) also operate.

FUSHIMI

SAKE BREWERIES IN FUSHIMI

Fushimi is one of the most famous sake brewing towns in Japan. Fushimi's groundwater consists of well-balanced minerals, including potassium and calcium, making it ideal for sake brewing. Fushimi's sake brands are made with this excellent water, using the long-kept traditional brewing methods of each local brewer. These are known for their mild taste and smooth texture.

There is an area where the beautiful antique sake warehouses from the Meiji period are standing side-by-side, and it is ideal for a stroll. You can find museums in the remodeled warehouses, and gift shops selling the brewers' own sake selections. Visiting the traditional sake breweries and learning of the depths of this ancient craft may make you love it more.

❸ GEKKEIKAN OKURA SAKE MUSEUM
月桂冠大倉記念館

247 Minamihama-cho, Fushimi, Kyoto
075-623-2056
www.gekkeikan.co.jp/english/products/museum/index.html

Gekkeikan is a historic sake brewery founded in 1637 in Fushimi. They have a museum in a renovated Meiji-period sake warehouse. The atmosphere of an old sake warehouse is recreated in the museum, where guides explain the sake brewing process in an easy manner. You can also visit the inside of a working sake brewery by appointment. They also offer a *kikizake* (sake tasting) of several different brands, including Ginjo-shu, a premium sake.

❹ KIZAKURA KINENKAN (KIZAKURA SAKE MUSEUM)
黄桜記念館

228 Shioya-machi, Fushimi, Kyoto
075-611-9921

This museum shows videos of the sake brewing process and displays brewing equipment. They also operate a restaurant where you can drink sake specially made for this restaurant or locally brewed beer.

❺ FUSHIMI INARI TAISHA
伏見稲荷大社

68 Fukakusa Yabunouchi-cho Fushimi,
Kyoto
075-641-7331
inari.jp

Among all of Kyoto's many splendors,
Fushimi Inari is especially breathtaking.
Set on a mountain on the southern
outskirts of the city, Fushimi Inari is a
Shinto shrine dedicated to Inari, the god
of rice. It dates back to the early eighth
century, and has counted Toyotomi
Hideyoshi among its many patrons.

What makes the shrine truly remarkable
are the thousands upon thousands of
torri gates that line its meandering paths
like vermillion ribbons. The gates, each
inscribed with messages honoring donors,
wind their way up the mountain—a
daunting three-hour climb to the top
rewards travelers with stunning vistas and
endless discoveries of torii-lined paths
and small shrines, many dotted with small
foxes (symbols of *kitsune*, the messenger
of Inari). Along the way, small restaurants
offer souvenirs and treats (many fox
themed) to hungry travelers.

The shrine can be reached by the JR Nara
Line Inari Station or the Keihan Main Line's
Fushimi-Inari station. It is an important site
for New Year celebrations, drawing over
a million people each year, and is popular
with tourists throughout the year. Visit
at the end of the day to explore the trails
without the crowds as the sun sets over
Kyoto.

WHERE TO SEE

Yasaka Shrine

❻ MARUYAMA PARK
丸山公園

Maruyama-cho, Higashiyama-ku, Kyoto

Maruyama is the most famous park
in Kyoto. It was originally part of the
grounds belonging to Yasaka Shrine.
Within the vast grounds, there is
a bandshell, as well as the famous
Gion-shidare weeping cherry tree, which
attracts many visitors during the cherry
blossom season. During the night, the
cherry tree is lit up and is especially
gorgeous. The original weeping cherry
tree died in 1947 and the current tree has
replaced it in this spot.

At the eastern side in the park, there
is a statute of Sakamoto Ryoma and
Nakaoka Shintaro. Ryoma is standing,
holding his head high and Shintaro is on
one knee next to Ryoma. It was originally

made in 1934, but melted down for
resources during WWII. The current
statute was remade in 1962.

❼ KYOTO RYOSEN GOKOKU SHRINE AND THE RYOSEN HISTORY MUSEUM
京都霊山護国寺/霊山歴史館

1 Seikan-ji Ryozen-cho,
Higashiyama-ku, Kyoto

Located at the south of the Kodai-ji
Temple, the Kyoto Ryosen Gokoku
Shrine was established by Emperor
Meiji's suggestion in order to console
the spirits of those activists who died
without witnessing the Meiji Restoration.
There are the tombs of Sakamoto
Ryoma, Nakaoka Shintaro, and other
fallen activists of the Meiji Restoration,
and there is an endless line of visitors.
On Ryoma's memorial day, November
15, they hold Ryoma-sai ceremony and
shamo-nabe (hot pot with game fowl) is
served, because Ryoma and others were
preparing to eat shamo-nabe for dinner
the day that they were killed.

SAKAMOTO RYOMA

Across the street from the shrine is the Ryozen Museum of History. It is also known as Bakumatsu-ishin Museum, and it displays the historical material and literature regarding the end of the shogunate era and the Meiji Restoration. The museum has collected over 5,000 materials, including Ryoma's mementos, of which about 100 articles are on permanent exhibition. They often hold special exhibitions on different subjects.

Ryoma's Tomb at the Ryosen Gokoku Shrine

❽ SUYA
酢屋

Kawaramachi Sanjo-sagaru,
Nakagyo-ku, Kyoto
075-211-7700

❽ AKEBONO-TEI
明保野亭

2-222 Kiyomizu, Higashiyama-ku, Kyoto

Near the Ryozen Gokoku Shrine, Akebono-tei, a traditional Kyoto-style restaurant, is located on Sannen-zaka Slope, which heads towards the famous Kiyomizu-dera Temple. At the end of Edo period, Akebono-tei was operating as a restaurant and inn where Ryoma and other activists would often stay or have meetings. Photos of Ryoma are displayed at the entrance. Bento box meals with tofu and *yuba* (tofu skin) are popular. There is also a meal of assorted dishes called Ryoma Gozen. You can enjoy this traditional Kyoto-style meal in a compact bento box from between 2,000 and 3,000 yen, which is a reasonable price range for this famous tourist area.

When the last shogun was turning over rule to the emperor, Ryoma was staying at a lumber shop called Suya in Kawara-machi Sanjo. The owner of the shop was a supporter for Ryoma and had let him hide out on the second floor. Suya's building still has the atmosphere from Ryoma's time, and the first floor is now a woodcraft shop and the second floor is a gallery called Gallery Ryoma. The street in front of the shop is also known as Ryoma-dori (Ryoma Street).

Suya

KYOTO'S HANAMACHI (PLEASURE QUARTER) FOR THE ACTIVISTS: SHIMABARA
島原

The Big Gate of Shimabara

Many people may associate Kyoto with geisha. Geisha and *maiko* (apprentice geisha) normally work in pleasure districts like Gion, Kami-shichiken and Miyagawa-cho. These areas are called *hanamachi* (flower town) where visitors are entertained by singing and dancing. Since the early Edo period, there have been six hanamachi in Kyoto, and of those, Shimabara was most associated with the activists of the late Edo period.

In Shimabara, not only partying but also Japanese traditional literary arts such as *waka* or *haikai* poetry were popular. In the mid-Edo period, the Shimabara Poetry Circle was formed and played a central role in Kyoto culture.

The most popular image of the Kyoto geisha may come from Authur Golden's 1997 novel and movie, *Memoirs of a Geisha*, which was set in Gion. Shimabara was a little different from Gion mainly from the fact that there were *tayu* working in Shimabara.

A tayu was the highest rank for women who entertained guests at parties. They were skilled in singing and dancing, but also highly skilled in other cultural disciplines, including tea ceremony, flower arrangement, and waka and haikai poetry. Shimabara's tayu were awarded very high rank from the court, which was equivalent of the level of *daimyo* (feudal lord). Shimabara tayu were not like courtesans at all.

Shimabara was home to the two types of business: high-end Japanese-style restaurants or banquets halls called *age-ya* and *cha-ya* where the clients could have private parties with tayu, and *oki-ya*, which employed both tayu and geisha. In other words, oki-ya managed stars like tayu, while age-ya and cha-ya offered the setting and produced the show. This system is still maintained in other hanamachi like Gion today.

However, due to its unfavorable location and other reasons, Shimabara gradually lost its popularity since the Meiji period, and it closed its business as a hanamachi in 1977. Today, only the "Big Gate of Shimabara," which was rebuilt in 1867, remains as a sign that this was ever a hanamachi.

Shimabara *tayu*

SAKAMOTO RYOMA

Sumiya Motenashi Art Museum

⑩ SUMIYA MOTENASHI ART MUSEUM
角屋もてなしの文化美術館

32 Nishi-shinyashiki-ageya-cho,
Shimogyo-ku, Kyoto
075-351-0024
www16.ocn.ne.jp/~sumiyaho/page/
english.html

Sumiya was an *age-ya*, which was founded in 1641. The activists of the late Edo period would gather here in secret; Ryoma is known to have been here. The building is now registered as Important Cultural Property and you can visit inside the Sumiya Motenashi Art Museum. It is an exceptional place to learn about the culture of the time.

Open: March 15–July 18,
September 15–December 15
Viewing the second floor requires
advance reservation and separate fee.

⑪ WACHIGAIYA: 320 YEARS OF HISTORY IN SHIMABARA
輪違屋

114 Nishi-shinyashiki-nakano-cho,
Shimogyo-ku, Kyoto

Today, Wachigaiya is known to be the only place left to have *tayu* employed. It was established in 1688 and is still in business operating as both an *age-ya* and *oki-ya* in Shimabara. It often appears in novels set in the late Edo period. The current building was rebuilt in 1857 and is of cultural note. You cannot look inside unless you visit as a customer. They only accept regulars, therefore it is not easy for a tourist to see inside.

WHAT IS A GEISHA?

Literally meaning artist, or performing artist, a geisha is a woman trained to entertain by song, dance, calligraphy, reciting verse, and conversation. There are many misconceptions surrounding geisha, including that geisha engage in prostitution. Typically, geisha do not engage in sex for money, even though they are adeptly skilled in flirtation and innuendo. The misconception likely stemmed during WWII, when prostitutes referred to themselves as geisha girls to the American GIs. It takes years of training, often starting at a young age, to be considered a geisha. Geisha are said to occupy another reality, *karyukai*, the flower and willow world. In Kyoto a geisha is generally called a *geiko*.

WHAT IS A MAIKO?

A *maiko* is a geisha in training. In Tokyo, maiko are called *hangyoku* and usually start training at 18; in Kyoto, at 15. Maiko are trained by *onee-san* ("older sister") in the proper ways of serving tea, how to play the shamisen, dancing, casual conversation, and more. The onee-san also help pick the maiko's geisha name.

HOW TO MEET A GEISHA

You would be very lucky if you run into a real geisha or maiko on the streets of Kyoto. (Unfortunately, you may think you saw one, not knowing it was just a Japanese visitor dressed as a maiko for cosplay). It is very rare to see a real one on the street.

The sure way to meet them is to set up a party to hire them. However, most *cha-ya* do not accept first-time customers. You can ask a regular customer to take you, but finding a regular customer is not easy. (Most Japanese people will never go to such places in their lives.) Also, having a private party in hanamachi is very expensive. However, in recent years, some cha-ya have opened bars on the premises where you can walk in and experience the hanamachi atmosphere. There are some bars where you can even ask for geisha or maiko to sit with you.

You may try Bon-ton in Miyagawa-cho. In summer, Kamishichiken Kaburenjo Theatre, near Kitano-tenman-gu Shrine, turns into an exotic beer garden, where maikos in *yukata* (casual kimono for summer) serve customers. It offers you a special evening in Kyoto at a reasonable price.

BON-TON
ぽんとん
4-321 Miyagawa-suji, Higashiyama-ku, Kyoto
075-551-2436

KAMISHICHIKEN KABURENJO
上七軒歌舞練場ビアガーデン
742 Shinsei-cho, Kamigyo-ku, Kyoto
075-461-0148

SAKAMOTO RYOMA

MAIKO EXPERIENCE

STUDIO SHIKI
スタジオ四季
www.maiko-henshin.com/english

AYA
彩
kyoto-maiko.com/English
Many other businesses offer similar
services.

If you are interested in becoming a *maiko* or getting dressed like one, you may want to look into packages that offer dress, make-up, and professional photography in the range of 12,000 to 13,000 yen and up (for about 2 hours). There are many packages available. For example, you can pay the company to take you to a scenic place and photograph you, or you can select a package where you can dress up as a samurai.

KYOTO

KYOTO SCENES

Clockwise, from top: Miyako Orori at Gion; Yasaka Pagoda; Nishiki Market; Bamboo Grove in Sagano

Clockwise, from top left: Kiyomizudera; Yudofu; Heian Jingu Shrine; Kamo River; Kyo-kaiseki; Manpukuji in Uji

Shibuya Crossi

東京

TOKYO

View of Shinjuku with the Fuji Mountain

KAWAII & COOL: World-Exclusive Tokyo Culture

Tokyo races along the cutting edge, with its history as a constant companion. Such a contradiction is second nature to the nation of Japan, the so-called mysterious country of the East. And at Japan's center lies its capital, Tokyo.

It's a city that meshes a chaotic Asian character with the refinement of Paris and New York. It might bring to mind the Ridley Scott film *Blade Runner*, which was inspired by Shinjuku, or Sofia Coppola's *Lost in Translation*, with its commanding view of Tokyo's glittering nightscape from The Park Hyatt Tokyo.

Costume girls in Shibuya

Vending machines lined up like a modern art installation; subways running on a meticulous schedule; people, waves and waves of people, streaming over Shibuya's huge multi-way intersection. And then you find, like a sanctuary nestled between rows of office buildings, a small, traditional temple or shrine. Where there's kabuki theater, with men playing female roles, there's also the Takarazuka Revue, with women playing the men. Everything must seem so strange and wondrous to the eyes of an outsider—even the smiling, cosplay girls handing out fliers in Akihabara, seemingly plucked straight from the screen.

Orderly, immaculate, and stylish, but also seedy, kitschy, and chaotic. That's Tokyo, and there's no other city in the world quite like it. Here we'll show you just the tip of its many attractions.

T O K Y O

JR Chuo Line

ART

1 NEZU ART MUSEUM

2 TARO OKAMOTO MEMORIAL MUSEUM

3 SUNTORY MUSEUM OF ART

4 ROPPONGI HILLS

5 THE NATIONAL ART CENTER TOKYO

6 UKIYO-E OTA MEMORIAL MUSEUM OF ART

7 PRADA AOYAMA STORE

8 TOKYU PLAZA OMOTEDANDO

9 OMOTESANDO HILLS

ANIME EXPERIENCE AND OTAKU CULTURE

1 HELLO KITTY SHOP

2 POKÉMON CENTER MEGA TOKYO

3 GUNDAM BASE TOKYO

4 KIDDY LAND

5 MITAKA NO MORI GHIBLI MUSEUM

6 CAMPUS MUSASHINO

7 AKB48 CAFÉ & SHOP AKIHABARA

8 MAID CAFES

9 AKIHABARA PASELA SHOWA STREET HOUSE

10 GUNDAM CAFÉ

11 KAIYODO "HOBBY LOBBY TOKYO"

CLASSIC AND POPULAR

1 KABUKI-ZA

2 SHINBASHI ENBUJO THEATER

3 NATIONAL THEATRE

4 HAMA-RIKYU GARDENS

5 KOISHIKAWA KORAKUEN GARDEN

6 ASAKUSA AND SENSO-JI TEMPLE

7 ASAKUSA HANAYASHIKI

8 KAPPABASHI DOGU STREET

9 KAGURAZAKA

10 THE IMPERIAL PALACE

11 TOKYO SKYTREE TOWN

12 TOKYO TOWER

13 TSUKIJI / TOYOSU FISH MARKET

14 EDO TOKYO MUSEUM

15 TOKYO MIZUBE CRUISING LINE WATER BUS

16 OOEDO ONSEN MONOGATARI

Temple   Shrine

JAPAN'S WILDLY VARIED CULTURAL ATTRACTIONS, FROM MUSEUMS AND GARDENS NURTURING THE TRADITIONAL JAPANESE ARTS TO THE VIVID CONTEMPORARY ART SCENE

❶ NEZU ART MUSEUM
根津美術館

6-5-1 Minami-Aoyama, Minato-ku, Tokyo
03-3400-2536
www.nezu-muse.or.jp/en/

Aoyama is an especially stylish neighborhood, even for Tokyo. The Nezu Art Museum sits serenely amid the clusters of high-fashion flagship stores like Prada, Chloé, Jil Sander, and Comme des Garçons. Here you can appreciate at your leisure the pinnacle of classic Oriental paintings, ceramics, tea sets, arms and armor, and more. The building, renovated by the architect Kuma Kengo in 2009, is a work of art in itself

Businessman and art collector Nezu Kaichiro built the museum on the former site of his home, as a place to display his collections. Of special note is the extensive traditional Japanese garden. It boasts four tea rooms and is dotted with Buddha statues and stone lanterns. Here, time drifts by at a calmer pace than you would ever expect in the middle of this busy metropolis. A first-time visitor would be surprised to find such a sprawling garden remaining here in Aoyama, where real-estate prices tend toward the astronomical. The garden even has a café, Nezu Café, where you can soak up the verdant beauty while enjoying tea and snacks. Many visitors

Nezu Art Museum

ART

come just for a stroll in the garden. It's a great spot to catch your breath from shopping in Aoyama. Don't miss the museum shop, which offers stationery and other original merchandise featuring designs from the museum collections.

The collection of over 7,000 pieces includes highlights like the Ao-Ido tea bowl that Oda Nobunaga gave to his close vassal, Shibata Katsuie, as well as seven acknowledged national treasures. One of those treasures, Ogata Korin's famous *Irises* painting, is on display every year from the latter part of April through the first couple weeks of May.

❷ TARO OKAMOTO MEMORIAL MUSEUM
岡本太郎記念館

6-1-19 Minami-Aoyama, Minato-ku, Tokyo
03-3406-0801
www.taro-okamoto.or.jp/en/

Okamoto Taro (1911-1996) was a luminary in the world of contemporary art. The building that served as his home and studio from 1954 for over 40 years is now open to the public as the Taro Okamoto Memorial Museum. Viewed from outside, it blends right into the surrounding residences. But once you step inside, you see Okamoto Taro's distinctive figure sculptures and

Taro Okamoto Memorial Museum

exquisitely designed chairs scattered around the garden. The studio, with artwork left in place, still pulses with energy. You can't fail to be sucked in to this world, your senses overwhelmed.

Okamoto Taro worked in both abstraction and Surrealism. Many of his works bear an influence from primitive art. In 1930, he pulled out of the Tokyo University of the Arts and spent about ten years living with family in France. He attended the Sorbonne, studying subjects as eclectic as philosophy and ethnology, until he came across some of Picasso's work in a gallery. The effect on him was tremendous; the story is that he threw himself into painting with the stated goal of outdoing Picasso. He coined the popular Japanese adage "Art is an explosion!" and was known far and wide for his fresh and unusual performances. His masterpiece, the *Tower of the Sun*, was used as the symbol of the 1970 World's Fair in Osaka.

TOKYO

MYTH OF TOMORROW MURAL
「明日の神話」

Okamoto Taro believed that art is something everyone should have access to. Fulfilling this credo, he has public art works installed in seventy spots around the country. Probably the largest and most widely viewed of these is *Myth of Tomorrow*, installed in the Shibuya Mark City Building, in the passageway between the JP Shibuya train station and the Keio-Inokashira line Shibuya station.

Myth of Tomorrow was commissioned by the owner of a hotel in Mexico, and created between 1968 and 1969. The hotel never opened, though, and the work remained unseen. It was discovered in Mexico in 2003, restored in Japan, and unveiled as a public artwork in Shibuya in 2008.

The painting is 18 feet (5.5 meters) tall and 98 feet (30 meters) across, and depicts the 1954 detonation of the hydrogen bomb by American forces at Bikini Atoll. The fishing ship Daigo Fukuryu Maru was bathed in nuclear fallout from the blast. The work is viewed as a picture of the resilience of people overcoming a tragedy. So powerful is the message from his painting that the timing of the 2011 Fukushima nuclear disaster, a replay of that nightmare—on the same year as Okamoto Taro's hundredth birthday—seemed like more than a coincidence.

❸ SUNTORY MUSEUM OF ART
サントリー美術館

Tokyo Midtown Galleria 3F, 9-7-4
Akasaka Minato-ku, Tokyo
03-3479-8600
www.suntory.com/culture-sports/sma/index.html

Inside Tokyo Midtown, a landmark development built in Roppongi in 2007, sits the Suntory Art Museum. Managed as a cultural outreach project by whisky brewer Suntory, the museum is based around the concept of "beauty in everyday life." It collects artworks that embody the immemorial, delicate Japanese aesthetic, as well as imported *nanban* (Portuguese and Spanish) fine arts from the Momoyama period.

The history of the Suntory Art Museum traces back to 1961. The museum changed location twice before making a new start in Roppongi in 2007, in a

ART

TOKYO MIDTOWN
東京ミッドタウン

Tokyo Midtown, Roppongi's newest hot spot, is a multi-use establishment featuring offices, shops, restaurants, rental apartments, the Ritz-Carlton Tokyo, an art museum, Billboard Live Tokyo, and a medical center. The complex is distinguished by its nine palatial acres of greenery, and a design that incorporates traditional Japanese aesthetics. The aim is to express the extraordinary sensitivity and hospitality of the Japanese people. The ornate Christmas-light display each year also attracts plenty of visitors.
www.tokyo-midtown.com/en

Among the shops of Tokyo Midtown are a good number that deal in traditional Japanese sundries and interior goods, like chopsticks and *zori* sandals. The traditional Japanese goods are redesigned in a modern way in order to adapt to Western-style living; there are as many ways to enjoy them as there are customers.

A must-see is the design shop THE COVER NIPPON, which combines traditional and modern sensibilities (Galleria 3F www.thecovernippon.jp). The store's point of pride is that its wares are made in Japan. Accordingly, its stock is made up of items that employ traditional Japanese crafts and materials. They include stylish fabrics, furniture, housewares, utensils, stationery, and household accessories. With items ranging from Nambu ironware teapots to USB flash drives lacquered with gold leaf, these items epitomize the concept of art in everyday life. Their beauty, backed by their skilled craftsmanship, utility, and design, wins them popularity among local shoppers and foreigners alike.

building designed by architect Kuma Kengo. The space is a comfortable, designed around the idea of "modern wa" (*wa* is a term that refers to things of traditional Japanese character), fusing Japanese traditions with modernity. Also housed in the museum is the Genchoan tea room, a bit of a hidden gem. The tea room was created alongside the museum in 1961. Following the museum's move to Roppongi, the tea room got a modern redesign that incorporated building materials from the original tea room, including pillars, sliding screens, and ceiling.

The tea room is not open for general viewing, but there is a ceremonial tea boiling that is open to the public every other Thursday, excluding holidays. The cost is 1000 yen for tea and seasonal sweets; museum admission is charged separately. Attendance is capped at fifty visitors a day, and once the sweets run out, the room is closed for the day. A demonstration of tea ceremony etiquette takes place at 1:00, 2:00, and 3:00 p.m. Enjoy the stately, ritualistic world of the tea ceremony in this atmosphere of Japanese refinement and hospitality.

❹ ROPPONGI HILLS AND THE ART & DESIGN STORE
六本木ヒルズ

Roppongi Hills West Walk 3F
6-10-1 Roppongi, Minato-ku, Tokyo
03-6406-6280
www.mori.art.museum/en/shop/

Roppongi Hills is host to offices and over two hundred shops and restaurants. At its heart is Mori Tower, whose 52nd and 53rd floors house the genre-spanning art exhibitions of the Mori Arts Center Gallery and the Mori Art Museum. And once you're in the tower, the Tokyo City View viewing platform on the 52nd floor presents another irresistible temptation. It affords a 360-degree view of Tokyo, which is especially stunning at night. The tableau presented by the Tokyo

Suntory Museum of Art

ART

Roppongi Hills Observatory

megalopolis could be considered art in its own right. There's a restaurant and a café, so you can spend some time here comfortably. (The price is 1500 yen; admission to the Mori Art Museum is included, but the Sky Deck above costs an extra 300 yen. roppongihills.com/tcv/en/)

Also recommended is the Roppongi Hills Art & Design Store, which sells original merchandise from contemporary artists. The offerings include cute items featuring Planet66, Murakami Takashi's original Roppongi Hills mascot; Kusama Yayoi's pumpkin-themed glass decorations, keyrings, and cookies; and candies in the motif of Nara Yoshimoto's girl drawings. All in all, it provides a more casual way to enjoy art. Sweets from globally renowned artists can make great souvenirs or gifts for the ones back home.

Roppongi Hills

OTHER MUST-SEE SPOTS

❺ THE NATIONAL ART CENTER TOKYO
新国立美術館

7-22-2 Roppongi, Minato-ku, Tokyo
03-5777-8600
https://www.nact.jp/

The building has a striking glass façade that undulates like a wave. This posthumous work by Kurokawa Kisho, Japan's ambassador to the architectural world, opened in 2007. It's the biggest and most luxurious exhibition space in the country, although it has no permanent collection. Begin with the exhibitions in the two main rooms, which can be historical or contemporary art from Japan and around the world such as Kusama Yayoi, Miyake Issei and Ando Tadao to Titan, Renoir and Modigliani. Then check out the smaller complementary exhibitions, from painting, prints, crafts and calligraphy to a variety of Japanese art and sculpture. Afterward, try one of the four restaurants and cafes—don't miss the tea salon, Salon de Thé Rond, in the shape of an inverse cone, then go to the museum shop on the first basement level for souvenirs from Tokyo. Here you can buy original merchandise created in collaboration with art director Sato Kashiwa, who also designed the museum's logo.

❻ UKIYO-E OTA MEMORIAL MUSEUM OF ART
浮世絵太田記念美術館

1-10-10 Jingu-Mae, Shibuya-ku, Tokyo
03-3403-0880
http://www.ukiyoe-ota-muse.jp/eng

One step off the main drag of Harajuku, a youth hotspot, is a small museum dedicated to the *ukiyo-e* art form of woodblock printing and paintings. Ukiyo-e was a populist art form in the early part of the Edo period. However, from the end of that period on into the Meiji era, ukiyo-e works started being exported *en mass* into the West, influencing artists such as Vincent van Gogh and Claude Monet. Businessman Ota Seizo, lamenting that state of affairs, spent over half a century collecting ukiyo-e art. He amassed approximately 12,000 pieces, of which a themed selection is displayed each month. There are even works from the masters of the form, Ando Hiroshige and Katsushika Hokusai. Surprisingly, many Japanese people aren't even aware that there is such an art museum in Harajuku. The museum may actually have a higher profile among foreign visitors than among native Japanese.

Top to bottom: *Kabuki Actor, Ichikawa Ebizo,* Toshusai Sharaku, 1794 ; Ukiyo-e Ota Memorial Museum of Art

TOKYO

135

MODERN ARCHITECTURAL HIGHLIGHTS

❼ PRADA AOYAMA STORE
プラダ

5-2-6 Minamiaoyama, Minato-ku, Tokyo

This building, made of diamond-shaped glass blocks, is a standout even amid the abundance of unique architecture in the Omotesando area. Swiss architecture firm Herzog & de Meuron, which also worked on the Tate Modern, did the store's design. The store is a mind-blowing sculptural work that stands like a piece of modern art itself. Just nearby is the Comme des Garçons Aoyama store, another true original with its use of blue cone shapes made of glass (designed by the London-based Future Systems).

❽ TOKYU PLAZA OMOTESANDO
東急プラザ 表参道原宿

4-30-3 Jingumae, Shibuya-ku, Tokyo

This fort-like shopping complex, located at the intersection of Omotesando and Meiji-dori, has the most amazing entrance. Ride the escalator up (or down) and you'll be enveloped into a kaleidoscope of mirrors that will surely throw you off balance. Designed by award-winning architect Hiroshi Nakamura and completed in 2012, the shopping complex's multifaceted entranceway looks like something out of a science fiction movie.

Tokyu Plaza

ART

❾ OMOTESANDO HILLS
表参道ヒルズ

4-12-10 Jingu-mae, Shibuya-ku, Tokyo

Well-known architect Ando Tadao worked on the retail and residential complex Omotesando Hills. What makes this three-story building distinctive is the way it was designed to harmonize with the rows of gently sloping Japanese zelkova trees framing it. The building has a low profile, but also extends underground to comprise six levels in all, with a spiral walkway ringing the interior of the building.

The Shibuya station of the Tokyo Metro Fukutoshin line, designed around the theme of "a spaceship floating underground," is an Ando design as well.

Omotesando Hills

WHAT IS KAWAII?

Kawaii (pronounced ka-wai-i) roughly translates to cute or loveable, but it can mean a lot more than that. It's a certain type of non-threatening, youthful cuteness—think smiling cartoon characters—that has become popular all over Japan with everyone from the teen girls who started the phenomenon to big business.

EXPERIENCE COOL JAPAN

❶ HELLO KITTY SHOP
ハローキティ・ショップ

For the Hello Kitty Tokyo station shop, exit the JR Tokyo station on near the central ticket gate on the Yaesu side. The Haneda Airport location of Hello Kitty Japan is on 5F of the Haneda Airport International Terminal. There is another location on 4F of the Tokyo Skytree Town Solamachi.

The cat character Hello Kitty was created in 1974, and her appeal remains eternal. If the world's most famous mouse is Mickey Mouse, then Kitty must be its most famous feline. Celebrities from Mariah Carey to Lady Gaga have professed their love for Kitty, and it's not uncommon to see her in crossovers with famous brand labels.

From that celebrity a shop specializing in Hello Kitty goods was born. The Hello Kitty Tokyo station shop is located on Tokyo Character Street, which connects to the Yaesu exit of the Tokyo train station. Roughly 1,200 items are for sale in this store, with its cute, overwhelmingly pink, interior design. The space is compact, but the draw is its proximity to the Tokyo station. Other character-based shops line Tokyo Character Street, dedicated to characters like Snoopy and Miffy.

Another location is the Hello Kitty Japan Haneda Airport shop, in the international terminal of Haneda Airport. Here an international traveler can find a full selection of items that would make good gifts for friends and family back home. There are original items you can't find anyplace else, like cream *daifuku* (rice cakes stuffed with sweet filling) shaped like Kitty's face. The cakes are so cute it feels a pity to eat them. The combination of Kitty and traditional Japanese sweets seems a bit surreal— and this, you might say, is the essence of Japanese *kawaii* culture.

❷ POKÉMON CENTER MEGA TOKYO
ポケモンセンター
メガトウキョー

Sunshine City alpa 2F, 3-1-2
Higashi-Ikebukuro, Toshima-ku
03-5927-9290
www.pokemon.co.jp/gp/pokecen/
english/

For fans of Pokémon and the lovable character Pikachu, the Pokémon Center Mega Tokyo is not to be missed. The Pokémon Center is Pokémon's official store, where you can buy all kinds of exclusive merchandise, including video games, the Pokémon Trading Card Game, figurines, plush characters, toys, and stationery. The store also hosts events like Pokémon TCG tournaments. On days when the store has exclusive video game character launches, the store gets mobbed with eager collectors.

The Pokémon Center Mega Tokyo is located near the Ikebukuro station, one of Tokyo's most famous tourist areas. It should definitely be on the itinerary of any Pokémon fan, and is a perfect place to pick up gifts for children and friends.

Pokémon Centers are located in Sapporo, Sendai, Skytree Town (Tokyo), Tokyo-Bay (Chiba), Yokohama, Nagoya, Kyoto, Osaka, Hiroshima and Fukuoka. You can also find smaller, more casual Pokémon shops in various locations, which offer a selection of the most popular products found at the main store.

TOKYO

Pokémon Scene,
©2018 Pokémon

Gundam statue in the Plaza at Diver City Tokyo

ANIME EXPERIENCE

❸ THE GUNDAM BASE TOKYO
ガンダム・ベース・東京

Diver City Tokyo, 1-1-10 Aomi, Koutō-ku
www.gundam-base.net

In 2009, a 59-foot-tall (18-meter) "actual size" Gundam made its debut in Odaiba, Minato-ku. During the 52 days it was on display, an estimated 4.15 million people came to see it. The memory is still fresh of a country gripped by Gundam fever.

Now, in the Plaza at Diver City Tokyo in Odaiba, you can enjoy the exhibition of a new Gundam, a life-sized unicorn Gundam statue. In the same building you will also find Gundam Base Tokyo, an official complex of Gunpla (a plastic model of Gundam) that opened in 2017 for Gunpla fans worldwide, and the Gundam Café.

❹ KIDDY LAND
キディランド

6-1-9 Jingu-mae, Shibuya-ku, Tokyo
03-3409-3431
www.kiddyland.co.jp/harajuku/

Kiddy Land stocks character merchandise of all kinds, from Hello Kitty and Mickey Mouse to the latest cartoon characters. It's a treasure trove of character merchandise, and ground zero for the latest toy trends. There are locations in each region of Japan, but the one you want to see is the primary location, founded in 1950 and an Omotesando landmark to this day. In Japan, world leader in mascot characters, everything from food to historical castles gets the mascot and merchandising treatment. Try to find your own favorite characters here.

TOKYO

WEST TOKYO

Director Miyazaki Hayao and his studio, Studio Ghibli, are the jewels of Japanese animation. At the Ghibli Museum, Mitaka, you can dive into the fantastic worlds of Studio Ghibli's films.

⑤ GHIBLI MUSEUM, MITAKA
三鷹の森ジブリ美術館

1-1-83 Shimorenjaku,
Mitaka, Tokyo
(inside Inokashira Park)

By advance reservation only
www.ghibli-museum.jp/en/

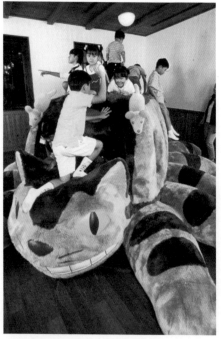

Cat Bus at Ghibli Museum

Director Miyazaki's works have influenced a generation of creators. The list begins with John Lasseter and runs through the ranks of Disney, Pixar, and more. From *Spirited Away*, the 75th Academy Award winner for Best Animated Feature, to *Ponyo* and more, Ghibli's films play across Asia and the West, attracting many fans outside of Japan. *Kiki's Delivery Service* is a classic standby to many American children. Studio Ghilbi director Yonebayashi Hiromasa's film *The Secret World of Arrietty* opened across America in 2012.

From Tokyo station, it's 30 minutes by train to the Mitaka JR station, then 5 minutes by bus to the museum. Beloved children's character Totoro greets you at the door. Even getting your entry ticket is fun; it's a real 35mm film cell, and you can hold it up to the light to see what's on it. There are frescoes on the entrance ceiling, a spiral staircase, and open-air hallways. Every aspect of the building's design makes you feel like you've wandered into a Studio Ghibli film. With thoughtful elements like a passageway that only children can fit through, you can feel Miyazaki's fingerprints all over the museum.

ANIME EXPERIENCE

The permanent exhibition includes copious wall displays of sketches and recreations of the animators' rooms, all giving you a look into the process of creating a Ghibli film. Also not to be missed are the museum-exclusive short films. The popular draw for children will be playing with the Catbus from *My Neighbor Totoro*. Another, more hidden, gem is the rooftop garden. Here, a 16-foot-tall (5 meter) robot warrior (from the film *Castle in the Sky*) stands silently, the museum's guardian spirit. Take a moment to just stand amid the greenery and enjoy the gentle breeze under the robot warrior's auspices. The museum also houses a shop selling character merchandise, and a café called the Mugiwara-bōshi ("Straw Hat") café.

The graffiti wall at Campus Musashino

❻ CAMPUS MUSASHINO
武蔵野カンプス

I.G. Building 1F, 2-1-9 Naka-cho, Musashino, Tokyo
0422-36-6218

This authentic pizzeria serving delicious, affordable eats is a popular restaurant. But few customers realize that its parent company is a famous animation studio known for producing Oshii Mamoru's *Ghost in the Shell* and the animated segments of *Kill Bill: Vol. 1*. The building housing the restaurant is itself the headquarters of that studio: Production I.G.

The animation elements are toned down in the service of making it a regular, go-to neighborhood hangout, but the walls are festooned, graffiti-like, with autographs and drawings from famous animators. From *Ghost in the Shell* characters to the eponymous hero of Naruto, wildly popular even in America, the wall is lined matter-of-factly with illustrations that are sure to make their fans smile. You may come across the animators or directors having meetings there. At a five-minute walk from the north exit of the Mitaka station, it's a bit far from the center of Tokyo, but for Production I.G. fans and lovers simply of Napolitan pizza, it's a worthwhile stopover on the way home from the Ghibli museum. The wood interior is warm and welcoming.

TOKYO

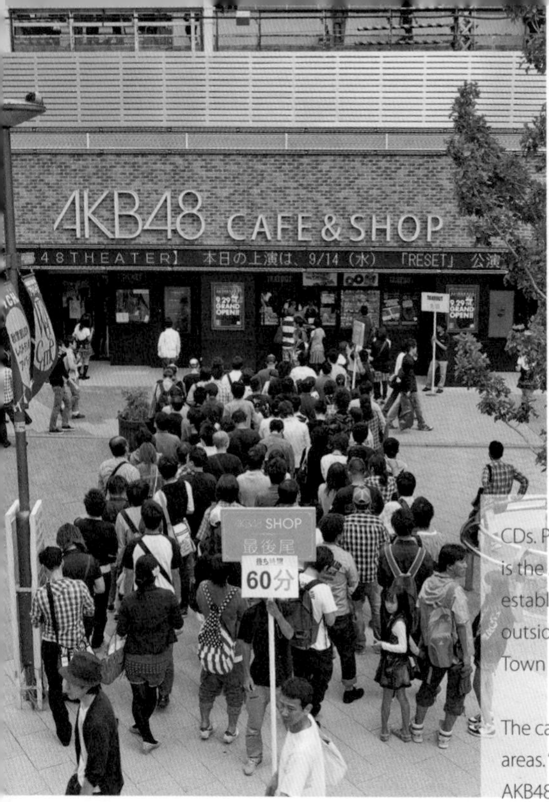

AKIHABARA: MYSTERIOUS TOWN THAT FUSES OTAKU AND KAWAII

⑦ AKB48 CAFÉ & SHOP AKIHABARA
AKB48 カフェ&ショップ 秋葉原

1-1 Kanda Hanaoka-cho, Chiyoda-ku
03-5297-4848
akb48cafeshops.com/wp/akihabara/english

AKB48 is a pop idol group that comes from Akihabara (so named because AKB is an acronym for Akihabara, and the group has 48 members). The standing stage here is attended by devoted fans every day. The group is a veritable phenomenon, enjoying nationwide popularity and releasing million-seller CDs. Plugged right into this boom is the AKB48 Café & Shop Akihabara, established in 2011 and located right outside the Akihabara JR station Electric Town exit, next to the Gundam Café.

The café is split into theater and café areas. "Idols you can come meet" is AKB48's catchphrase, but the group's wild popularity ensures that concert tickets are hard to come by. So here in the café's theater area, you can take in a performance video while also taking in a meal. At the café area you can enjoy a menu devised by members of the group.

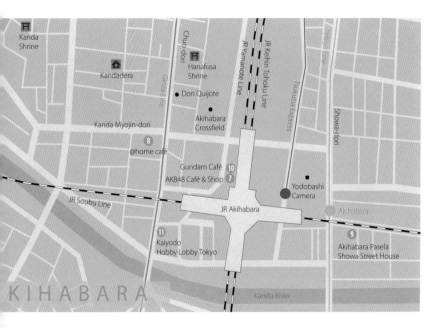

KIHABARA

AKB48's schoolgirl-ish outfits might make the uninitiated Westerner think the group is some kind of middle-school amateur-hour act (member ages actually range into the mid-20s). But in Japan, that kind of nonprofessional air is part of the appeal. Perhaps it really hits the spot for fans of so-called *moé* anime. You won't find actual AKB48 members at the café, but the smiling waitresses seem like they could be back-up members. Each coaster features an image of an AKB48 member (you never know which one you'll get). More fan-pleasing features are signatures and messages, in the group members' own handwriting, decorating the tables and sofas. You can find AKB48 donuts and other exclusive merchandise in the associated shop. All in all, it's the perfect place for a field study of Japan's idol culture.

⑧ MAID CAFES
メイドカフェ

@home café
4th–7th floors Mitsuwa Building
1-11-4 Sotokanda, Chiyoda-ku
4F Tel: 03-3255-2808
5F Tel: 03-5294-7709
6F Tel: 03-5294-7708
7F Tel: 03-5294-7707
www.cafe-athome.com/en/

The latest craze to sweep Akihabara is the maid café. Now, "maid" in this case doesn't mean an actual domestic servant. The "maids" here are costumed waitresses. There do exist maid cafés that are relatively restrained. But the ones that get the most media play are the ones built like a theme attraction, where costumed girls who look like they're

Maid Café in Akihabara

straight out of manga comic books greet you with a florid "Welcome home, Master!" (*Okaerinasaimase, goshujin-sama!*) This is the new *moé* culture, which has drawn media coverage from as far away as *The New York Times*. It's a virtual space where customer and employee can enact the roles of master and maid.

The @home café chain (pronounced "at home"), which has five locations in Akihabara alone, is a fully realized entertainment café. The chain has an established protocol; when you enter the café, instead of saying, "*Irasshaimase*," (welcome), the employees say, "Welcome home, Master." ("Mistress" in the case of female customers.) When you leave, instead of saying, "Thank you very much," they call out "Please have a good trip, Master." The cafés aren't very

spacious, but, surprisingly, the chain employs 180 maids.

The maids all have the appearance of pop idols, and seem like collectable figures come to life. A conspicuous presence inside the café is that of the male regulars who show up to see a particular favorite maid. Thanks perhaps to the over-the-top, on-bended-knee service, some people have the mistaken idea that a maid café is some kind of adult shop. But the actual atmosphere is squeaky-clean. It's not rare to see couples or groups of women in attendance. It's an audience-participation kind of place, where you can take your picture or play a game with a maid (with a fee for each activity). Every time a drink is served, the maid and customer chant together, as if reciting a magical incantation, "Moe moe, shaka, shaka, love injection. Be tasty!" Let yourself be pampered here without reservation.

Foreigners are known to visit from time to time, so each location has a maid who speaks English. The hand towelettes are printed with "Welcome home, Master," in English, Korean, Chinese, French, Spanish, and so on. You can also get a membership certificate, called a "License of Your Majesty," certifying your master status.

The above is just one example type of maid café. Along with the spread of maid cafes has come a proliferation of themes and amenities. For instance, there is a café that calls itself the Sengoku Maid Café (Warring States Maid Café), where servers wear period Japanese garb (with license taken to allow for a miniskirt), and a Butler Café, where male butlers serve female patrons on bended knee. The food and drink are only a bit more expensive than at a normal café, so you could call this a reasonable way to experience a truly "foreign culture."

WHAT IS MOÉ?

Moé is a slang expression denoting the romantic feeling, affection, or deep obsession one has towards imaginary characters. Today, the term is used widely to express feelings for real women, idols, animals, or things.

Moé in Akihabara

⑨ AKIHABARA PASELA SHOWA STREET HOUSE
秋葉原パセラ昭和通り館

2-10 Sakuma-cho Kanda, Chiyoda-ku
0120-706-738
www.pasela.co.jp/shop/akihabara

Karaoke, which translates to "empty orchestra," is a Japanese-born phenomenon. It has now spread to every country of the world, but it's still worthwhile to see what developments it has undergone back in its birthplace. The karaoke box has evolved; there are now specialized karaoke bars for solitary karaoke. Special amenities have proliferated. There are now places where you can sing in your own private room while enjoying a foot bath, or where you can rent a free cosplay costume.

The Akihabara touch is embodied in Akihabara Pasela Showa Street House, where you can sing your heart out in rooms designed around popular anime and games. The rooms are designed from top to bottom to fit various themes like *Monster Hunter*, *Evangelion*, and *Sengoku Basara*. You can taste the thrill of being a hero or heroine. (Room themes are subject to change.) The character figures lined up as decoration are catnip to fans. Even the menu displays a sense of humor. Reservations are required for the most popular rooms.

⑩ GUNDAM CAFÉ
ガンダム・カフェ

1-1 Hanaoka-cho Kanda, Chiyoda-ku
03-3251-0078
g-cafe.jp/en/

"Electric Town" Akihabara (or Akiba), otherwise known as the *otaku* Mecca, is a gathering place for *otaku* (obsessive fans) of anime, computers, and other geeky pursuits. It is likewise a favorite of tourists from abroad. And since 2010, Akihabara has had a new hot spot. Below the overpass right outside the train station you'll find the Gundam Café, a theme café based on the popular robot animated TV show and films *Mobile Suit Gundam*. Thanks to its clean, white, near-future interior design, even those of the non-*otaku* persuasion will enter without having to be dragged inside.

That being said, the visitor who ducks inside mistaking it for a Starbucks is in for a bit of confusion. The place contains a cornucopia of fan bait, from menu items named after characters to displays of classic Gunpla (Gundam plastic models). You'll also find 59-inch (150 cm), 1:12 scale models of the Gundams themselves (which are supposed to be 59 feet [18 meters] tall in "real life."). Even the bathroom is an experience. Push a special switch, and the lights flicker and you hear the booming sounds of a Gundam activating. It feels like you've stepped into Gundam's cockpit.

Mobile Suit Gundam is a long-running animated TV series that started airing in 1979. Popular not just in Japan but all over Asia, the franchise has grossed an estimated $1.2 billion. There's always a new series coming out on the heels of the last one, and there are ten theatrical feature films and counting. You might write off *Gundam* as just another dime-a-dozen kid's show about robots fighting to save humankind, but you'd

be mistaken. The franchise claims many passionate adult fans. Fans say that the first series, especially—now referred to as "First Gundam"—is a gripping human drama in a richly realized world, with strong elements of realism drawn from World War II. The result is the not-infrequent sight of a father from the "Gundam generation," the core of the fandom, explaining the stories to his grade-school-age child.

The customers are a diverse lot, split about 50/50 between passionate *Gundam* fans and those who come

in just to say they've been. You can buy "Gunpla-yaki," grilled cakes in the shape of a Gunpla (and apparently at 1/144 actual scale). The gift shop is fully stocked with other exclusive items like chocolates and sweets with images from *Gundam*.

⑪ KAIYODO "HOBBY LOBBY TOKYO"
海洋堂「ホビーロビー東京」

Radio Kaikan 5F, 1-15-16 Sotokanda, Chiyoda-ku
03-3253-1952

Kaiyodo is a world-famous plastic modeling company, foremost in the world in modeling design and techniques, and revered in the modeling world. Its influence stretches as far as the film *Jurassic Park*, whose staff used Kaiyodo models as reference in creating its dinosaurs, and the American Museum of Natural History in New York, which ordered models from Kaiyodo for display. In Japan, a lot of people beyond just collectors know about the little models that come bundled with some packaged candies. These pack-ins, rather than being considered secondary to the candy, boast exquisite quality that makes them a target for adults.

Hobby Lobby Tokyo in Akihabara is Kaiyodo's sole outlet store in Japan. Samples of new merchandise are displayed here, and events of all kind are held. There are also displays of merchandise that used to be sold, so you can look through the shop as you would a kind of Kaiyodo gallery.

Aside from model figures of animals, military ships, and anime characters, the

Spider-Man action figure by Kaiyodo

Akihabara street scene

goods here include poseable figures of Pixar animated characters like Woody and Nemo, and elaborate models of Transformers (seen recently in the Hollywood film adaptations). Causing a big stir recently is the line of poseable Buddhist action figures, which, it's safe to say, are the first of their kind. The lineup includes Ashura, Vaisravana, and more (3800 yen). The minute detail and beauty of these figures is quite arresting. They would make for Japanese souvenirs with a definite cool factor.

You should also make sure to see the line of Tokyo Landmark models, miniatures of sites like the Asakusa Kaminari-mon, the Tokyo Skytree, and the National Diet Building (available for sale exclusively at the official store in the Tokyo Skytree). The quality is high, but the reasonable price of 420 yen is sure to please.

Kabuki scene

EXPERIENCE THE
TRADITIONAL JAPANESE ARTS

APPRECIATING KABUKI
歌舞伎

1 Kabuki-za
歌舞伎座
4-12-15 Ginza, Chuo-ku, Tokyo
03-3541-3131
www.kabukiweb.net/theatres/kabukiza/

2 Shinbashi Enbujo Theater
新橋演舞場
6-18-2 Ginza, Chuo-ku
03-3541-2600
www.kabukiweb.net/theatres/
shinbashi/

3 National Theatre
国立劇場
4-1 Hayabusa-cho Chiyoda-ku
03-3265-7411
www.ntj.jac.go.jp/english/access/
facilities_01.html

Just as a tourist in New York will want
to take in a Broadway musical, many
tourists in Japan will want to enjoy the
traditional theatrical arts of Japan. The
type of Japanese theater most familiar to
foreigners is probably *kabuki*. Kabuki is a
form of theater that combines elements
of drama, dance, and music. It has
remained in active development over its
long 400-year history, readily absorbing
influences from *bunraku* puppet theater
and other fads and trends along the
way. (Of course, compared to *Noh*

CLASSIC AND POPULAR

theater, with its 600-year heritage, kabuki is a relative newcomer.) This is a form with classical roots, but even today it continues to push the envelope with projects like new Shakespeare adaptations.

Kabuki may look intimidating from the outside, but even a superficial appreciation will afford pleasures in the form of lush, elaborate sets, costumes and striking makeup. People with any interest in Japanese kimono should definitely check it out. Some productions boast spectacles like rapid onstage costume changes and performers suspended in midair. The show is made far more accessible to English speakers with the use of English-language audio guides that explain the text and plotlines. The truth is, even Japanese people have a hard time understanding the language in kabuki. It's hard for non-experts to gain much fluency. The result is that a lot of people hold a token respect for kabuki without really understanding or appreciating it. It's probably similar to opera in that respect.

Playhouses specializing in kabuki can be found in Tokyo, Kyoto, and Osaka. The most famous is the Kabuki-za theater in Ginza, Tokyo. Established in 1889 and carrying on a proud tradition of over 120 years, the Kabuki-za is a beloved Ginza landmark. The building of the theater itself, renovated thoroughly in the spring of 2013, with its classical Japanese architecture, is a popular spot for tourist photos.

There are also other theaters close by that mount kabuki plays, such as the Shinbashi Enbujo theater and the National Theatre. Each location has a different program and company, so it's a good idea to check the English-language Kabuki Official Website at www.kabuki-bito.jp/eng/top.html before you go. The website is full of useful information and program guides that will help you appreciate the shows. You can also find an interview about kabuki with Peter Gelb, general manager of the Metropolitan Opera in New York. The site also links to other sites where you can buy performance tickets online.

TOKYO

Renovated Kabuki-za

JAPANESE GARDENS
日本庭園

Surprisingly enough for a city filled with rows and rows of office buildings, Tokyo has a lot of greenery. Some of that is in the form of traditional Japanese gardens. One step inside a Japanese garden, an atmosphere of peace and calm floats over you, letting you forget the hustle and bustle of the city. There's more to enjoy in a Japanese garden than just the seasonal blooming of the apricot and cherry blossoms. The scenery is landscaped to resemble mountains and lakes, and the result is quite arresting. It feels like you're looking into a giant painting. Basically, these are not just gardens, but works of art to experience. When you're worn out from shopping, take a breather in a Japanese garden and see for yourself what truly distinguishes it from Western gardens.

Several gardens in the heart of Tokyo used to be part of famous estates. The most centrally-located and easily-accessible of these are Hamarikyu Gardens and Koishikawa Korakuen Garden. There are also hotels and wedding halls whose grounds contain gardens that make up in elegance what they lack in size. Good ones to see are Chinzanso and Happo-en. These sites also house restaurants and cafés. Happoen's garden houses a tea room, where you can enjoy the matcha tea ceremony. If you can, definitely try a stroll during the cherry-blossom and foliage seasons.

HAMA-RIKYU GARDENS
浜離宮恩賜庭園

KOISHIKAWA KORAKUEN GARDEN
小石川後楽園

CHINZANSO
椿山荘
10-8, Sekiguchi 2-chome, Bunkyo-ku
03-3943-1111
www.chinzanso.com/english

HAPPO-EN
八芳園
1-1-1 Shirogane-dai, Minato-ku
03-3443-3111
www.happo-en.com/english/garden

Happo-en

Hama-rikyu

TOKYO

④ HAMA-RIKYU GARDENS
浜離宮恩賜庭園

1-1 Hamarikyu-teien, Chuo-ku
03-3541-0200
teien.tokyo-park.or.jp/en/hama-rikyu

Hama-rikyu is a famous garden that embodies the Edo era sensibility. Its saltwater lake, Shioiri-no-ike, is fed by the ocean and waxes and wanes with the tides. This feature makes the garden unique; there is nothing like it even in Kyoto, as Kyoto does not face the ocean. In the spring, a field of rape blossoms unfurls in front of the Shiodome office skyscrapers. This strange pairing is the very much in character for Tokyo.

The shogun used this land for falcon hunting in the latter half of the 17th century. After that, Matsudaira Tsunashige, younger brother of the fourth shogun, Tokugawa Ietsuna, re-appropriated the land to build a home. Upon the ascension of his son, Tokugawa Ienobu, as the sixth shogun, the site came to be used as a villa for the shogun's family. At that time it was called Hama Goten, meaning beachfront villa. Since the shogun's primary residence was in Edo, the Hama-rikyu Gardens site was essentially a beachfront getaway for his personal use. The gardens were maintained by successive shoguns down the line. After the Meiji Restoration, the site came to be used as an imperial villa, and acquired the name Hama-rikyu, meaning beachfront palace. After World War II, the garden was granted to the Tokyo metropolitan government, and after renovation it opened to the public for an entrance fee, which goes toward the cost of maintaining the garden.

Attractions here include the peony garden, comprising about 800 plants of 60 different varieties, and a 300-year-old pine tree planted during the reign of the sixth shogun. The flower garden blooms with rape blossoms in the spring and with cosmos in the fall. During cherry blossom season, the garden is lit up after dark for nighttime viewing. There is also a tea house in the middle of the pond called Nakajima no Ochaya, (meaning, appropriately enough, "tea house on the central island") where you can enjoy the cool of the evening or appreciate the moon's beauty, drinking green tea while you gaze out onto the pond and the bridge. Take some tea and consider yourself a personal guest of the shogun.

⑤ KOISHIKAWA KORAKUEN GARDEN
小石川後楽園

1 Koraku, Bunkyo-ku, Tokyo
03-3811-3015
teien.tokyo-park.or.jp/en/koishikawa/

Koishikawa Korakuen Garden was planted on the grounds of the Mito Tokugawa estate in 1629, in the early Edo period. The Mito family was a major branch of the Tokugawa family, and produced many shoguns. Korakuen Garden was finished during the rule of Daimyo (Lord) Tokugawa Mitsukuni. Mitsukuni, also called Mito Komon, is mostly known today as the eponymous hero of the nationally broadcast television drama *Mito Komon*. His story—he travels the nation in disguise, clearing out wrongdoers—is at least vaguely familiar to a lot of Japanese people. They call this garden "Komon's Garden."

Hama-rikyu

CLASSIC AND POPULAR

The garden has a pond in the center, ringed by a footpath. It is notable for the Chinese flavor of its landscape design, filled with scenic elements that recall the picturesque Chinese landscape. The scenery is rich in variety, with deft landscaping that evokes lakes, mountains, rivers, and fields. Of particular beauty are the 60-year-old weeping cherry tree and the autumn foliage.

Next door are the Tokyo Dome, an indoor stadium seating 55,000, and the Tokyo Dome City amusement park. These couldn't be more different in character from the serene Korakuen Garden. With such variety, the area is often bustling with young couples and families. It's an entertaining contrast to note.

TOKYO

Koishigawa Korakuen

Kaminari-mon at Senso-ji

STREETS WITH SPIRIT: ENJOY JAPANESE ATMOSPHERE IN ASAKUSA & KAGURAZAKA

❻ ASAKUSA AND SENSO-JI TEMPLE
浅草、浅草寺

2-3-1 Asakusa, Taito-ku
03-3842-0181
www.senso-ji.jp/about/index_e.html

Nakamise-dori
www.asakusa-nakamise.jp/e-index.html

The Asakusa area boasts unwavering popularity among overseas tourists. At its heart is Senso-ji, a temple to the Buddhist goddess of compassion, Kannon. This is the oldest temple in the city, with a history reaching back to the 7th century. It was a major temple where feudal lords came to pay their religious duties. In the Edo period, Tokugawa Ieyasu made it into a place where people could offer prayers for the shogunate government, and it thrived while occupying a central space in Edo culture. Today, approximately 30 million people come on pilgrimage each year.

The symbol of Senso-ji is the Kaminari-mon, or Thunder Gate. You can't miss its huge red lantern. Statues of wind god Fu-jin and thunder god Rai-jin stand on either side and fix you with a steely glare. This is a spot that invites photography, and you'll find it teeming with tourists. Flanking the path into the shrine is the famous Nakamise-dori, a shopping arcade where souvenirs and

CLASSIC AND POPULAR

sweets are sold just as they were in times of old. This is one of the oldest shopping areas in Japan, and possibly your best bet if you're looking to buy things that scream "Japan."

❼ ASAKUSA HANAYASHIKI
浅草花やしき

2-28-1 Asakusa, Taito-ku, Tokyo
03-3842-8780
www.hanayashiki.net/en

On your way back from Senso-ji, you might enjoy a stop at this amusement park steeped in working-class warmth and charm. Asakusa Hanayashiki is Japan's oldest amusement park. First established in 1853 as a botanical garden, the park was destroyed during the Pacific War, and rebuilt in 1947. It could fairly be called the Coney Island of Japan, and that analogy holds even down to the later decline of both parks.

Nakamise-dori at Senso-ji

Hanayashiki's most popular attraction is probably its roller coaster. Built in 1953, it's the oldest coaster in Japan, and is still in active duty. And just like Coney Island's Cyclone, this one also looks ready to fall apart any second. Riding the coaster is a thrill from top to bottom, as you even seem to graze the side of a neighboring building (all constructed for show, of course).

There is also an outdoor stage, called "Oedo Stage," in the Hanayashiki-dori shopping district right outside the amusement park proper. You don't even have to go into the park to enjoy a free and fun ninja show. The ninja action heats up every hour, on the hour, during weekends and holidays.

TOKYO

Senso-ji

ANNUAL EVENTS IN ASAKUSA

Asakusa's most well-known festival is probably the Sanja Matsuri (Festival) in May. The festival is held from the third Friday of the month to the following Sunday. People parade a *mikoshi* portable shrine around the city, accompanied by vigorous shouting. Approximately 1.5 million people gather in this 700-year-old tradition over the entire course of the festival.
www.asakusajinja.jp/english/

Indelibly associated with summer in Tokyo is the Sumida River Firework Festival. This festival is held every year on the last Saturday of July, on the Sumida River at the edge of the Asakusa area. One million people jam the area, angling for a close view. This venerable tradition began in the 18th century, and is even depicted in *ukiyo-e* paintings from the Edo era. Over 20,000 individual fireworks are launched each year. The festival also serves as a contest for fireworks manufacturers, so the competition between them means viewers are usually in for some innovative, original pyrotechnic displays.

The people of Asakusa love novelty, and there's no better demonstration of that than the Asakusa Samba Carnival, established in 1981. It's an entertaining mashup of a samba parade and contest, like you'd find at the Carnival in Rio, with the unlikely surroundings of the Shitamachi area, still imbued with the atmosphere of Edo-era Japan. The costumes and dancing are set to rival even the real Carnival in Brazil. The beat and passion of samba just might have something to pass on to the sound of Japan's native festivals. The carnival is now a 30-year-old tradition indelibly associated with summer. It takes place each year on the last Saturday of August, and boasts about 500,000 participants.

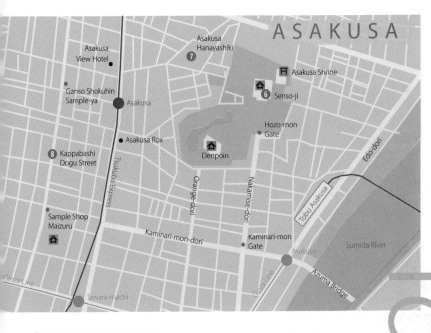

Asakusa Hanayashiki
Asakusa View Hotel
⑦
Ganso Shokuhin Sample-ya
Asakusa
Asakusa Shrine
⑥ Senso-ji
Hozo-mon Gate
Asakusa Rox
⑧ Kappabashi Dogu Street
Denpoin
Edo-dori
Orange-dori
Nakamise-dori
Tobu Asakusa
Sample Shop Maizuru
Kaminari-mon-dori
Kaminari-mon Gate
Sumida River
Asakusa
Azuma Bridge
Ginza Line
Ginza Line
Tsukuba Express
Tawara-machi

⑧ KAPPABASHI DOGU STREET
かっぱ橋道具街

GANSO SHOKUHIN SAMPLE-YA, IWASAKI BIAI, KAPPABASHI SHOWROOM
元祖食品サンプル屋
3-7-6 Nishi-Asakusa, Taito-ku
03-3841-1456
www.ganso-sample.com/en/
(There is another location in Tokyo Solamachi, at the Tokyo Skytree Town.)

SAMPLE SHOP MAIZURU MAIN STORE
まいづる本店
1-5-17 Nishi-Asakusa, Taito-ku,
03-3843-1686
www.maiduru.co.jp

This shopping district is home to about stores selling restaurant equipment. Most non-industry tourists come for the replica food samples, which are so elaborately detailed that one could mistake them for the real thing. Here's an item you don't see much of in the West. In Japan, food replicas are placed in the windows of old-fashioned Japanese restaurants in place of menus. No bones about it; just one glance tells you what kind of cuisine the restaurant serves. And specialty stores dealing in those replicas are what you'll find on Kappabashi Dogu Street.

Mini food-replica key rings and magnets are popular as souvenirs and gifts. The resemblance to a shrunken piece of sushi or cake is startling. They're all handmade, and each one is subtly different. These replicas are another Japanese art form with a history of over 80 years, so they hold quite an attraction for overseas tourists.

TOKYO SCENES

Clockwise, from top left: Edo figures and Kabuki scene at Edo Tokyo Museum; The Great Wave off Kanagawa by Hokusai at Tokyo National Museum; Meiji-Jingu; Kisenosato, a sumo wrestler; Water Jar (Shigaraki ware)

CLASSIC AND POPULAR

Clockwise, from top left: Chidorigafuchi; Tokyo JR station; a bird café; realistic plastic food sample display; life-size superhero model at Shinjuku Kinokuniya bookstore.

❾ KAGURAZAKA
神楽坂

CAFÉ-CRÉPERIE LE BRETAGNE
4-2 Kagurazaka, Shinjuku-ku
03-3235-3001
www.le-bretagne.com/e/top.html

KINOZEN
紀の善
Kinozen Building, 1-12 Kagurazaka,
Shinjuku-ku
03-3269-2920

TATSUMIYA
たつみや
4-3 Kagurazaka, Shinjuku-ku
03-3260-7016

CANAL CAFÉ
1-9 Kagurazaka, Shinjuku-ku
03-3260-8068
www.canalcafe.jp (Japanese)

Another area that retains the atmosphere of the Edo era is the elegant, stone-paved Kagurazaka neighborhood. Unlike Asakusa, Kagurazaka is not on the standard tourist itinerary. It is, however, a popular area for Westerners, especially French, residing in Japan. The closest JR station is Iidabashi station. Its easy accessibility, again in contrast to Asakusa, is another attraction.

Walk up the sloped road in Kagurazaka and you'll find Zenkoku-ji, temple to Bishamonten, worshipped since the Edo era. Old houses and converted restaurants line the labyrinthine stone alleyways surrounding the temple. It's nice to take a look at the stores selling Japanese traditional sundries. This is still an active *hanamachi* (geisha quarter), with restaurants hosting Kagurazaka geisha, adding a slightly sultry air.

Café-Créperie Le Bretagne

CLASSIC AND POPULAR

Zenkoku-ji

This district has an unspoiled Japanese character, but another distinguishing characteristic is the high number of French restaurants. There is always a crowd at créperie Le Bretagne, whose famous *galettes* (crepes made of buckwheat flour) can stand up to ones from Brittany. The green-tea *bavarois* served at famous café Kinozen are another attraction. Then there's the venerable Tatsumiya, a subdued and tasteful unagi eel restaurant visited by John Lennon and Yoko Ono. And on the bank of the canal, where the cherry blossoms can make a beautiful sight, there's the Canal Café, giving off a resort flavor.

TOKYO

Canal Café

The Imperial Palace

LEARN ABOUT THE IMPERIAL PALACE AT THE HEART OF TOKYO

⑩ THE IMPERIAL PALACE
皇居

THE EAST GARDENS OF THE IMPERIAL PALACE
皇居東御苑
Admission is free. The Gardens are closed on Mondays and Fridays. Entrances are at the Ote-mon gate, the Hirakawa-mon Gate, and the Kitahane-bashi-mon Gate.

www.kunaicho.go.jp/e-event/
higashigyoen02.html

MUSEUM OF THE IMPERIAL COLLECTIONS
三の丸尚蔵館
www.kunaicho.go.jp/e-event/
sannomaru02.html

The Imperial Palace is located in the heart of Tokyo. You might well call this expanse of greenery the Central Park of Tokyo, but what sets it apart is the fact that it's also where the Emperor lives. The Imperial Palace is an Edo-era castle that originally belonged to the Tokugawa Shogun. That's the reason it's enclosed in a moat. The imperial residence had been in Kyoto for over a millennium, but in 1869, Emperor Meiji moved the capital to Tokyo, which serves as the imperial residence to this day.

CLASSIC AND POPULAR

Even so, not many Japanese people could tell you precisely where on the grounds the ceremonial palace or the Emperor's living space is. The area around the former Western Citadel is normally off-limits for walk-ins, but you can apply beforehand for a study visit. Sightseeing tours lasting an hour and 15 minutes are held for the general public on weekdays, twice in the morning and afternoon. You can apply in English online to attend this course. Also, on January 2nd and on Emperor Akihito's birthday on December 23rd, the imperial family makes several appearances on the Chowa-den balcony. Anyone can come see these appearances, with no reservations needed. Guests enter at the main gate to the palace (the Niju-bashi).

Reservations for general sightseeing: sankan.kunaicho.go.jp/english/guide/koukyo.html

Sightseeing information: www.kunaicho.go.jp/e-event

Some portion of the huge Imperial Palace grounds is open as public parks. In the former Kitanomaru area (Northern Citadel), there is Nippon Budokan (a martial arts hall) and the National Museum of Modern Art, Tokyo, as well as a landmark stretch of cherry-blossom trees along the Chidori-ga-fuchi moat. The East Gardens of the Imperial Palace are an expansive park containing sights like the ruins of the Edo Castle tower and the outer stone wall. Also on-site is Sannomaru Shozokan (the Museum of the Imperial Collections), whose collection of approximately 9,500 imperial heirlooms is free to see.

TOKYO

Ote-mon and Museum of the Imperial Collections at the Imperial Palace

Hanzo-mon at the Imperial Palace

RUNNING AT THE IMPERIAL PALACE

RUNNING STATIONS:

Hanzo-mon Runners Satellite JOGLIS
FM Center B1, 1-7 Koji-machi,
Chiyoda-ku, Tokyo
03-3221-6100
www.joglis.jp/index.php

ADIDAS RUNBASE
Hirakawa-cho Mori Tower 1F, 2-16-1
Hirakawa-cho, Chiyoda-ku, Tokyo
03-3261-9980
adidas.jp/running/runbase

MARUNOUCHI BIKE & RUN
Shin-Marunouchi Building B1, 1-5-1
Marunouchi, Chiyoda-ku, Tokyo
03-6269-9806

The latest things to spring up around the Imperial Palace are the so-called Imperial Palace Runners, who like to jog around the palace perimeter. The location is growing in popularity among runners, owing to the beauty of the verdant greenery surrounding the moat, and to the course's lack of traffic lights. One lap is about 3 miles (5 km), and the difference in elevation ranges about 85 feet (26 meters). The site is a draw for both beginners and expert runners.

Many people come here to enjoy a jog either before or after work. Running stations to support these joggers have sprung up in series, offering showers,

CLASSIC AND POPULAR

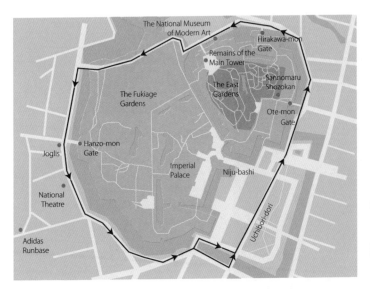

changing areas, and lockers where joggers can stash their bags. Institutions that charge a visitors' fee can, of course, also be used by sightseers. Policies vary among pay-per-use institutions, but you can expect a charge of about 500 to 800 yen. You can also rent bath towels and other accoutrements.

No small number of foreign celebrities has jogged the Imperial Palace, including President Bill Clinton. If you've already been to the palace to see the sights, challenging yourself to a run could be a memorable experience. The scenery during cherry-blossom season, especially, doesn't fail to impress. If you stay in a hotel convenient to the Imperial Palace running track, in the Marunouchi area for instance, you should be able to try it out with minimal fuss. Just try to observe good running etiquette and keep to a one-way circuit. This is especially important since congestion and pedestrians have become an issue, owing to track's recent boom in popularity.

Tokyo Skytree

Tokyo Skytree has viewing platforms at 1,150 and 1,475 feet up (350 and 450 meters). The entrance fee is a bit on the steep side, but the viewing platform boasts a number of delights, like a glass floor that lets you look down to the ground far below your feet. It feels like you're walking through the sky. Right near the tower are an aquarium, a planetarium, office buildings, and the Tokyo Solamachi shopping center comprising 310 shops and restaurants. The area, Tokyo Skytree Town, is practically a self-contained city in itself.

In keeping with its name, the Tokyo Skytree's design presents the appearance of a giant tree stretching into the sky. Made using classical Japanese artistic sensibilities and liberal use of cutting-edge technology, the Tokyo Skytree is a prized new landmark of Japan. Even the design of the lights at night, with their elegant muted purple and pale blue, reflects careful consideration towards harmonizing with the calm and ancient town scenery below it.

The tower is in Oshiage, Sumida-ku, in the Shitamachi area, at a slight distance from the center of Tokyo. The closest train station is the Tokyo Skytree

⑪ TOKYO SKYTREE TOWN
東京スカイツリータウン

1 Oshiage, Sumida-ku
www.tokyo-skytree.jp/english

In May of 2012, a new Japanese landmark was born, measuring 2,080 feet (634 meters) tall—the Tokyo Skytree, the new symbol of the city. The new radio tower is a successor to the 1,092-foot-tall (333-meter) Tokyo Tower. And, practical uses aside, it has also become a real hotspot for sightseers.

In keeping with its identity as "the number-one tower in the world," the

CLASSIC AND POPULAR

station on the Tobu Isesaki line, and the Oshiage station on the Tokyo Metro Hanzomon and Toei Asakusa lines. It's right near Asakusa, making them good to visit together in one trip. The contrast between the traditional neighborhood and this ultra-modern tower is striking.

⑫ TOKYO TOWER
東京タワー

4-2-8 Shiba Koen, Minato-ku
www.tokyotower.co.jp/english

Its stature may have been diminished somewhat by the debut of the Tokyo Skytree, but you still can't write off the appeal of Tokyo Tower, completed in 1958. The 1,092-feet-tall (333 meters) Tokyo Tower, lit up in orange and just edging out the 1,050-feet-tall (320-meter) Eiffel Tower, is an indispensable part of the Tokyo nightscape. On weekend nights, it's lit with a beautifully glittering diamond veil. The colors of the lights carry a message, with purple signifying dreams and blue signifying life.

In contrast with the Skytree in Shitamachi, the area here is a bustling shopping district with business and restaurants. It's located at a convenient distance from Roppongi, and has Tokyo skyscrapers lined up at its feet. Like the Skytree, the Tower's viewing platform has a glass "Look-down Platform" built into the floor, which lets you look at the ground 476 feet (145 meters) below. At the viewing platform café, you can take in a live music while admiring the nightscape.

Tokyo Tower

⑬ TOYOSU FISH MARKET
豊洲市場

6 Toyosu, Koto-ku
https://www.shijou.metro.tokyo.lg.jp/
english/toyosu/

Toyosu Market took over the wholesale fish business from the aging Tsukiji Market, and opened as the "new Tokyo's kitchen" for sushi, restaurants, and for the home on October 11, 2018, on the man-made island of Toyosu in the Bay of Tokyo. The new market is near Shijomae Station, on the Yurikamome Line, in Tokyo's Koto Ward—about 2km east of Tsukiji's old location.

The market is open from 5am to 5pm. The famous tuna auction takes place from about 5:30am to 6:30am. If you're happy watching from the upper-floor observation windows, you don't need to sign up beforehand. The auction can also be viewed from a special deck on the lower floor. Access to this deck is by application only, with applications open for about seven days each month, for a spot the following month. If you are lucky enough to get a place, you'll be assigned a 10-minute slot between 5:45am and 6:15am to see the auction action with a group of other people. A maximum of 120 people will be given access to the deck each day.

There are almost 40 restaurants here. Besides sushi shops, there is also a café, a tonkatsu joint and a curry shop to choose from. Then shop for souvenirs at Uogashi Yokocho Market—more than 70 shops sell specialties like nori (sea weed) and kanbutsu (dry foods). Go up to the rooftop garden early in the morning for views of Tokyo Bay.

CLASSIC AND POPULAR

GOURMET AND SHOPPING AT THE TSUKIJI FISH MARKET

Tsukiji Outer Market
築地場外市場
http://www.tsukiji.or.jp/english

The Tsukiji outer market, a collection of hundreds of shops and eateries selling everything from fresh seafood to cooking equipment, adjacent to the old inner market area, is not going anywhere.

This is an area where anyone can come and go freely. The place is lined with shops dealing in food, tableware, and cookware, as well as restaurants serving everything from sushi to rolled egg, pickled vegetables, and nori. It makes for a fun shopping experience all around. Keep in mind that many stores close early in the afternoon. Even if all you do is window-shop, it's worth a visit to soak up the atmosphere.

It may be a good idea is to check out the action at the Toyosu Fish Market first, in the early morning hours, and then head over to the old Tsukiji Outer Market—it offers more options than Toyosu for sushi (or other food) and shopping.

TOKYO

Tsukiji Outer Market

Scenes from Tsukiji Outer Market

TOKYO SCENES

Clockwise, from top left: Hie Shrine in Akasaka; Ginza; Shibuya Blue Cave in December; Shinjuku; Kabukicho, Shinjuku; Harajuku

⑭ EDO-TOKYO MUSEUM
江戸東京博物館

1-4-1 Yokoami, Sumida-ku
03-3626-9974
www.edo-tokyo-museum.or.jp/english/

The Edo-Tokyo Museum introduces visitors to the history and culture of Edo and Tokyo in all their dimensions. The nearest train stop is the Ryogoku station on the JR and Toei Oedo lines. It's right next to Ryogoku Kougi-kan, where sumo matches are held. The museum's permanent exhibits are divided into three parts, including "Edo Zone" and "Tokyo Zone." The exhibits feature life-size models of historical buildings, as well as *ukiyo-e* paintings and picture scrolls, clothing, ancient maps, and more.

Worthwhile sights are the life-size recreations, using the same original timber, of the early 19th-century Nihonbashi bridge, the Nakamura-za

kabuki playhouse, where productions were mounted in the Edo period, and the row houses where common people of the Edo era made their homes. The exhibit is built around items that give you a personal, tactile experience of what everyday life was like for regular people in Edo; you can cross the Nihonbashi bridge, and lift up a *senryobako*, a box filled with a thousand gold ryo oval coins to feel the heft for yourself. The Tokyo Zone has exhibits about the Meiji restoration and its Westernization movement.

The museum truly makes you feel like you've walked through a time portal into the Edo era, and is a delightful must-see for anyone with an interest in history. You can rent audio guides to hear explanations in English as you view the exhibits.

⑮ TOKYO MIZUBE CRUISING LINE WATER BUS
水上バス「東京水辺ライン

03-5608-8869
Regular service every day
www.tokyo-park.or.jp/waterbus/english/

Take a leisurely boat trip down the river. From Ryogoku or Asakusa to Odaiba,

Edo-Tokyo Museum

pass underneath bunches of bridges and get a unique angle on Tokyo. You might call this Tokyo's equivalent of the New York Circle Line or the Seine river Bateaux Mouches of Paris, although the water buses here pass mainly through the Shitamachi area, so you won't see many skyscrapers. During cherry-blossom season, though, the trees on the riverfront are the best ones to see. The trip from Ryogoku to Odaiba takes 55 minutes. There is also a night cruise where you can take in the delights of the evening scenery.

A view of the Rainbow Bridge and Tokyo Bay from Odaiba

16 OOEDO ONSEN MONOGATARI
大江戸温泉物語

2-6-3 Aomi, Koto-ku
03-5500-1126
daiba.ooedoonsen.jp/en/

Free shuttle bus from Tokyo station, Shinagawa station, and others. Admission includes towel and *yukata* rental.

Say you want to try going to an *onsen*, hot spring, but you don't have the time for a side trip to Hakone. Or you want to stay at a resort inn with an onsen, but you don't have the budget for it. In that case, maybe an onsen theme park, suffused with the spirit of onsen but located right in the heart of Tokyo, is just the ticket. Ooedo Onsen Monogatari, in Odaiba, is just such an establishment, designed with an abundance of authentic Edo feeling.

Upon entering, you change into your choice of *yukata* (a light, cotton kimono) and settle in. Then you can try out a variety of different baths, like a natural open-air bath, a sauna, or a footbath. If you're the type who's embarrassed to undress in front of strangers, you can enjoy a sand bath, and get buried in sand for a separate fee.

There is also shopping and eating, and attractions such as fortune tellers, making this a place where you can enjoyably spend the whole day.

TOKYO

Depa-chika at Daimaru Tokyo

DEPA-CHIKA (DEPARTMENT STORE BASEMENTS)
デパ地下

MITSUKOSHI GINZA
三越
4-6-16 Ginza, Chuo-ku
03-3562-1111
www.mitsukoshi.co.jp

ISETAN SHINJUKU
伊勢丹
3-14-1 Shinjuku, Shinjuku-ku
03-3352-1111
www.isetan.co.jp

DAIMARU TOKYO
大丸
1-9-1 Marunouchi, Chiyoda-ku
03-3212-8011
www.daimaru.co.jp/tokyo

SEIBU IKEBUKURO
西武
28-1-1 Minami-Ikebukuro, Toshima-ku
03-3981-0111
www2.seibu.jp/ikebukuro

TOBU IKEBUKURO
東武
1-1-25 Nishi-Ikebukuro, Toshima-ku
03-3981-2211
www.tobu-dept.jp/ikebukuro

Japanese department store basements, often abbreviated as *depachika*, are a wonderland of dining. You'll find huge delis stocked with ready-made dishes and boxed lunches of Japanese, Chinese, and Western cuisine; and you'll find dessert palaces chockablock with sweets, from Kyoto's pedigreed Japanese-style confectioners to famous French patisseries selling chocolate bonbons. These popular shops can be focal points for any department store to draw in customers, so they tend to get competitive with their wares. Among the must-sees are the Mitsukoshi department store in Ginza, Isetan in Shinjuku, Daimaru near the Tokyo station, and Seibu and Tobu in Ikebukuro. All the items at these stores are standouts, with an incredible amount of consideration going into each element of flavor and design. You're sure to find some good souvenirs and gifts along the way, such as the innovative lip-gloss-inspired "Sweet Lip" candy (525 yen) sold at the venerable confectionary Eitaro under its new label Ameya Eitaro (at Mitsukoshi Ginza and Isetan Shinjuku). Another fun suggestion for a day when the weather is nice is to pick up some ingredients at the depachika, and have lunch in the park.

YOSHOKU (OLD WESTERN-STYLE DINING)
洋食

RENGATEI
煉瓦亭
3-5-16 Ginza, Chuo-ku
03-3561-3882

GRILL MANTEN-BOSHI
グリル満点星
Main Location
Aporia Building B1, 1-3-1 Azabu-juban, Minato-ku,
03-3582-4324
www.manten-boshi.net/eng/

Few travelers are aware of the Japanese culinary genre of *yoshoku*, the Western-style meal, which is not Japanese cuisine, nor, exactly, Western cuisine. Fried prawns, rice omelets, hashed meat with rice, and pork cutlets are a few examples. This cuisine takes the essence and techniques of

Rice omelets at Rengatei

Western cooking and rearranges them in a Japanese style. It was created and developed back in an era when real French cooking was something that most people didn't have access to. The ideal is a high-quality dish in a casual context, and at a reasonable price. One distinctive feature is the inclusion of rice. It's a staple of home cooking, although what you'll find at the classic eateries, with their special sauce or recipes, is a little different. This is another unique Japanese flavor palate distinct from classic Japanese cooking, and well worth a try.

The well-known Ginza eatery Rengatei boasts a nearly 120-year history. Grill Manten-boshi Azabu-juban, with branches in Marunouchi and Shinjuku, is very accessible for tourists.

THE PEOPLE'S CUISINE: TRY YAKITORI AND YAKITON UNDER THE OVERPASS
焼き鳥

RASHOMON
羅生門
1-13-8 Shinbashi, Minato-ku
03-3591-7539

TONTON
登運とん
2-1-10 Yuraku-cho, Chiyoda-ku
03-3508-9454

Japanese sushi and tempura have been making major inroads in Western dining. But when Japanese people normally go out to eat with friends or coworkers, they pick a casual, low-key place like an *izakaya* (similar to a pub) or a *yakitori* (grilled chicken) joint. Most beloved by Tokyo's office workers is the bar district around Shinbashi. Note in particular the old-style bars lined up under the train overpass, they're reliably packed with men on their way home from work. Part of the appeal is the affordability; you can enjoy yourself for just 2,000-3,000 yen. For, say, a New Yorker or a Londoner, the feeling is probably analogous to coworkers in enjoying a quick drink on their way home from work. This is the best place to observe drunk,

Tonton

Rashomon

middle-aged Japanese businessmen grumbling about their bosses in their natural habitat.

Right under the overpass on your way out of the Shinbashi station Ginza exit, the old-timey Rashomon is open for business. Despite being nominally a pub, the place has no door or partition, and the smell and smoke of grilling *yakitori* blankets the street. It's a prototypically chaotic Asian atmosphere that stands in stark contrast to the refinement of the nightlife district Ginza right next door. The customers all chow down appreciatively on yakitori, which comes on skewers and is not quite like Western grilled chicken. A female foreigner would need some courage to enter here by herself. English won't get you anywhere here, so be prepared to order using body language. Ask for yakatori with *biiru* (beer); just don't forget to say *kudasai* or *onegai-shimasu* (please give me/us).

Near Yurakucho station, one stop from Shinbashi, there is an area under the overpass called Yakitori Street. Just as the name indicates, it's a place where you'll find a lot of yakitori joints clustered together. Beer cases are placed out on the street in place of tables in a breezy version of patio seating, and scores of red lanterns sway back and forth. Long-established favorite Tonton offers not only yakitori but its house specialty, *yakiton* (grilled pork). It has been operating here for 60 years, and is open during the daytime as well. Overseas tourists have recently become a not-uncommon sight here, possibly because of the famous Imperial Hotel and the Peninsula Tokyo Hotel nearby. All the places here are completely open-air, so you can preview the clientele and food from outside to find a place that catches your interest.

Ramen at Mampuku

THE PROFOUND WORLD OF RAMEN
ラーメン

Ramen could be called Japan's national comfort food. This noodle soup has its roots in China, and is beloved in Korea and other Asian countries, but Japanese ramen has developed some distinct characteristics of its own. At about 800 yen per bowl, it certainly can't be called cheap. Each establishment has its own original soup in the running, and passionate fans will come from far and wide for a bowl of their favorite. The success stories are dramatic; once word spreads about a place, the lines become never-ending. A Japanese ramen restaurant in Hong Kong even received a star in the *Michelin Guide Hong Kong & Macau 2011*. Be it ever so humble, there's nothing like ramen.

There are various soup stocks used for ramen, including *shoyu* (soy sauce), *miso* (fermented soy), *tonkotsu* (pork bone), and *shio* (salt). There are as many ramen joints as there are stars in the sky, and nearly as many different preferences, so it's no easy task to crown a number-one ramen restaurant. Here is our list of well-known places that are also accessible to travelers, to start you on your quest.

MAMPUKU
萬 福
2-13-13 Ginza, Chuo-ku
03-3541-7210

OTSUKAYA
大塚屋
TOU Building 1F, 3-2 Ichigayata-machi,
Shinjuku-ku
03-3269-0801

SORANOIRO
ソラノイロ
Blue Building 1B, 1-3-10 Hirakawa-cho,
Chiyoda-ku
03-3263-5460

IPPUDO
一風堂
www.ippudo.com
Ginza: Central Building 1F,
4-10-3 Ginza, Chuo-ku
03-3547-1010

Ebisu: Highness Ebisu, 1-3-13 Hiroo,
Shibuya-ku
03-5420-2225

Roppongi: Daini Odagiri Building 1F,
4-9-11 Roppongi, Minato-ku
03-5775-7561

Marunouchi: Marunouchi Brick Square
B1, 2-6-1 Marunouchi, Chiyoda-ku
03-3217-2888

SHINATATSU SHINAGAWA
品達　品川
3-26-20 Takanawa, Minato-ku
03-5475-7020
www.shinatatsu.com

TSUKE-MEN TETSU
つけめんTETSU
KIBI
きび
SETAGAYA
せたが屋
MOKO TANMEN NAKAMOTO
蒙古タンメン　中本
NANTSUTTEI
なんつッ亭
MENYA SHO
麺屋　翔
SHINSEN
神仙
YARO RAMEN
野郎ラーメン
NEW TANTAN MEN
ニュータンタンメン

and more

Shinatatsu

TOKYO

Tonkotsu Ramen at Ippudo

First, you might try the *chuka-soba*, the specialty of the classic Chinese cookery Mampuku, in Ginza. To this day, the restaurant maintains the consistent flavor it's had since its founding in 1929. The soup is a plain *shoyu* stock. This is ramen made the simple traditional way.

For ramen made with the special thick *miso* stock popular with the strong-flavor–loving youth, go to Otsukaya. This place, established in 2003, is so popular that a there's a constant line. The original location is near Ichigaya station, and there are branches in Takada-no-baba and Koenji.

Ramen-eating tends to have a masculine image, but 2011 saw the launch of a new place called Soranoiro, whose sense of style should be a welcome sight to female customers. The interior is made up like a café. The name is appended with "Japanese soup noodle free style," by way of explanation. And the menu is just as unique as you would expect from the phrase like that. This is far from the classic ramen; you can also get dishes like "veggie soba,"

with pasta-like noodles in a vegetable base, or a dish using mussels.

If *tonkotsu* ramen is your pleasure, head for Ippudo, with locations in Ginza, Ebisu, Roppongi, and Marunouchi, among many others in the city. The original location was in Hakata, but it's since become a nationwide chain. A New York location opened in 2008, followed by branches in Singapore, Seoul, and Hong Kong.

Under the overpass at the Shinagawa station is the Shinatatsu, a group of nationally famous ramen vendors in a row. At only about a minute walk from the Takanawa exit of the Shinagawa station, it's a very convenient location; it's the easiest to get to when you're taking the shinkansen. Inside are Tsuke-men Tetsu (serving noodles with a

Veggie soba at Soranoiro

creamy broth on the side), Kibi (Chinese soba with a mild flavor), Setagaya (shoyu and seafood broth ramen), Moko Tanmen Nakamoto (spicy miso ramen), Nantsuttei (tonkotsu ramen), and more. Here you can have a taste-off of what's been labeled the pinnacle of ramen.

CONVEYOR-BELT SUSHI FOR 100 YEN PER PLATE

KURA ZUSHI SHINAGAWA
くら寿司
Keio-Shinagawa Building 2F, 2-17-1 Konan, Minato-ku
03-6718-5610

Conveyor-belt sushi, *kaiten zushi*, has started to make inroads abroad. These are sushi restaurants for the masses, where a conveyor belt carries sushi dishes around and you can pick from them freely. Be careful; conveyor-belt sushi restaurants can vary widely in price. There are chains, though, where you can get authentic sushi for 100 yen a plate (and most plates have two pieces), and the quality leaves nothing to be desired. You can eat here without qualms on any count.

Unfortunately, what with Tokyo's high real-estate prices, there aren't too many of this kind of restaurant in the center of the city. But one example is Kura Sushi Shinagawa Station. It cuts costs with impressive use of technology, with integrated circuit chips on each plate monitoring the freshness of the food and allowing for automatic plate counting when it comes time to settle up. You're free to take as many dishes as you want. The place is usually packed with families and large groups, but it's worth a visit on your way to or from the *shinkansen*.

TOKYO

Kura zushi

TORAYA CAFÉ

TORAYA CAFÉ AOYAMA
Shin-Aoyama Building West building B1,
1-1-1 Minami-Aoyama, Minato-ku
03-5414-0141
www.toraya-group.co.jp/toraya-cafe/

Toraya, a traditional Japanese confectionary, can lay claim to a history that spans five centuries. It's famous enough that it even has a branch in Paris, but the newest venture for this venerable shop is the Toraya Café, which produces revolutionary sweets, marrying Eastern flavors and Western ingredients, like chocolate. One marquee attraction is its *an* paste, which presents Toraya's prized an, sweet red-bean paste, in the form of a jam. You'll also find other surprising combinations giving rise to gustatory delights, like a paste that mixes *matcha* green tea powder and white chocolate into a sweet white-bean base, and a fondant of azuki bean and cacao. The brand has a café and shop in Aoyama. You will also find Toraya Cafe An Stand, where you can enjoy *an* sweets in a casual setting, in Kita Aoyama (near Omote-Sando Station) and Shinjuku (NEWoMan Shinjuku 2F). They are definitely worth a try even for people who don't think they like Japanese sweets.

The beauty and variety of Japanese foods.

MICHELIN THREE-STAR RESTAURANTS IN TOKYO

Tokyo is a city whose cuisine is second to none, not even New York or Paris. Here you can have high-level cooking from different countries all around the world. As testament to that fact, Tokyo boasts 11 three-star restaurants listed in the 2020 Michelin Guide.

In terms of price level and atmosphere, a yakitori or ramen joint and a three-star restaurant are worlds apart, but the dividing line might be a fuzzy one. In general, high-class Western-style restaurants in Japan are less formal than the three-star ones in the West, and the dress codes are looser. And on the other side of the equation, even billionaires will stand on line for a famous ramen joint.

At the highest-ranked restaurants, there's a delicate art to the cooking and the environment, and it all can feel like an awe-inspiring religious ritual. Be prepared to spend 30,000 yen per person for a dinner; 60,000 yen if it's a particularly expensive restaurant. And don't forget to make reservations. Below is a list of all the three-star restaurants in 2020. Just be aware that certain Japanese restaurants, especially some sushi places, can seem intimidating or inhospitable to travelers, so you may not feel entirely comfortable if you can't get a regular to accompany you. And don't forget, just because a restaurant has three stars doesn't necessarily mean that English is well spoken there.

SUSHI

SUSHI YOSHITAKE
鮨 よしたけ
Brown Place 9F, 7-8-13 Ginza, Chuo-ku
03-6253-7331
http://sushi-yoshitake.com/

JAPANESE CUISINE

RYUGIN
日本料理 龍吟
Tokyo Midtown Hibiya 7F, 1-1-2
Yurakucho, Chiyoda-ku
03-6630-0007
http://www.nihonryori-ryugin.com/

KOHAKU
虎白
3-4 Kagurazaka, Shinjuku-ku
03-5225-0807

KAGURAZAKA ISHIKAWA
神楽坂 石かわ
Takamura Building 1F, 5-37 Kagurazaka,
Shinjuku-ku,
03-5225-0173
http://www.kagurazaka-ishikawa.co.jp/

DINING AND SHOPPING

KANDA
かんだ
3-6-34 Moto-Azabu, Minato-ku
03-5786-0150
http://nihonryori-kanda.com/
information/

KADOWAKI
かどわき
2-7-2 Azabujuban, Minato-ku
03-5772-2553

AZABU YUKIMURA
麻布 幸村
Yuken Azabu 3F, 1-5-5 Azabujuban,
Minato-ku
03-5772-1610

MAKIMURA
まき村
3-11-5 Minami-Oi, Shinagawa-ku
03-3768-6388

MODERN FRENCH CUISINE

QUINTESSENCE
カンテサンス
Garden City Shinagawa Gotenyama 1F,
Kitashinagawa 6-7-29, Shinagawa-Ku
03-6277-0090
http://www.quintessence.jp/

JOËL ROBUCHON
ジョエル・ロブション
Ebisu Garden Place, 1-13-1 Mita,
Meguro-ku
03-5424-1347
http://www.robuchon.jp/joelrobuchon

L'OSIER
ロオジエ
7-5-5 Ginza, Chuo-ku
03-3571-6050
http://losier.shiseido.co.jp/

TOKYO

Fugu (blowfish) Sashimi

Ginza Chuo-dori

GINZA / YURAKUCHO
銀座/有楽町

From European haute couture to big "fast fashion" retailers and long-established kimono stores, you'll find all kinds of fashion pulled together in Ginza. Ginza is the very model of a high-class shopping district. You could call it Japan's Fifth Avenue, and you could call it essential for any visitor to Tokyo who loves to shop.

The venerable Mitsukoshi and Matsuya department stores are well worth a visit. Also worthwhile might be the Uniqlo Ginza store, the largest shop in the world for this leading brand of low-cost basics. Off of the main street are kimono accessory shops and traditional confectionaries, keeping the flow of business alive just as they did back in the day. On the upper floors of the Gucci, Chanel, and Bvlgari shops are restaurants, cafés, and bars run by the brands. If you're looking to have a sophisticated time in a stylish environment, look no further than Ginza.

Fashion-conscious men should hit Hankyu Men's Tokyo department store, an entire store dedicated to men's fashion that opened in 2011.

You should check out the brand new huge Ginza Six, an upscale shopping center with a rooftop garden and art installation. For more luxurious shopping, try Tokyu Plaza Ginza and Mitsukoshi, which also has an airport-type duty free shop, Duty Free Ginza, for foreign visitors' convenience.

DINING AND SHOPPING

MITSUKOSHI
三越
4-6-16 Ginza, Chuo-ku
03-3562-1111
www.mitsukoshi.co.jp

MATSUYA
松屋
3-6-1 Ginza, Chuo-ku
03-3567-1211
www.matsuya.com/foreigner/
en/m_ginza/

UNIQLO GINZA
ユニクロ
6-9-5 Ginza, Chuo-ku
03-6252-5181
www.uniqlo.com

GUCCI
4-4-10 Ginza, Chuo-ku
03-3562-8111
www.gucci.com

CHANEL
3-5-3 Ginza, Chuo-ku
03-5159-5555
www.chanel-ginza.com

BVLGARI
Ginza Tower
2-7-12 Ginza, Chuo-ku
03-6362-0555
www.bulgarihotels.com/en-us/
tokyo-restaurants/ginza/

TOKYU PLAZA GINZA
東急プラザ銀座
5-2-1 Ginza, Chuo-ku
03-3571-0109
ginza.tokyu-plaza.com/en/

GINZA SIX
ギンザ・シックス
10-1, Ginza 6-chome, Chuo-ku
03-6891-3390
ginza6.tokyo.e.abf.hp.transer.com

HANKYU MEN
阪急メン
2-5-1 Yuraku-cho, Chiyoda-ku
03-6252-1381
www.hankyu-dept.co.jp/mens-
tokyo/english/

Ginza Six

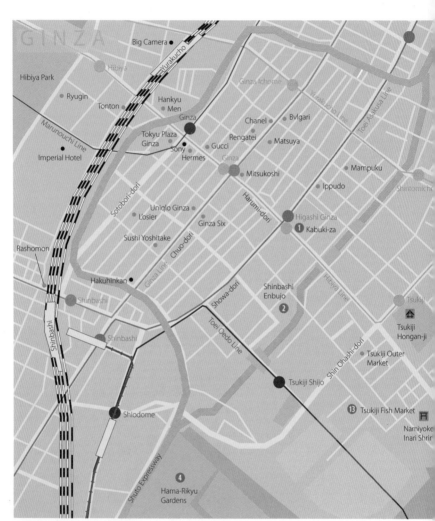

GINZA

銀座

HRAJUKU/
OMOTESANDO
原宿/表参道

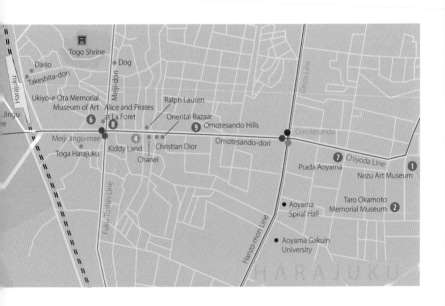

A group of friends walk along Takeshita Street in Harajuku

HARAJUKU / OMOTESANDO
原宿・表参道

Standing as a counterpoint to adult-oriented Ginza is Harajuku, the nerve center of fashion for the younger generation. From eye-catching fashions like the Lolita and Gothic Lolita to cool vintage threads, Harajuku has served as a pulse point for youth culture all over Japan, and even abroad. Designers and artists from around the world come to this district for inspiration in their work.

Takeshita Street, chockablock with shops offering cheap accessories and school uniform fashions, is mostly oriented towards teenage girls. Slightly older fashion-conscious youths, both male and female, flock to Cat Street, the main drag of Ura-Harajuku ("Backstreet Harajuku") and home to lots of edgy, idiosyncratic shops. You might enjoy a visit to some shops with Lady Gaga's own seal of approval, such as the second-hand clothing store Dog, and local label Toga, which she visited on a trip to Japan. Also, in the Harajuku landmark building Laforet Harajuku, you can find Lolita fashion shops like Alice and the Pirates. (There are sister branches called Baby, the Stars Shine Bright in Paris and San Francisco.) Lined up on one side, bordering on Omotesando with its beautiful rows of zelkova trees, are stores like Chanel, Christian Dior, and Ralph Lauren. This eclectic feeling is Tokyo in a nutshell.

If you're looking for some convenient souvenirs or gifts, head for the Oriental Bazaar, a popular spot for overseas tourists. When you get worn out from shopping, you can turn toward Meiji Shrine. Once you're on the palatial grounds, the clear air and serene atmosphere waft over you, and the hustle and bustle outside starts to feel like a dream.

DINING AND SHOPPING

DOG
Trinity Building B1, 3-23-3 Jingu-mae,
Shibuya-ku
03-3746-8110

TOGA HARAJUKU
Mansion 31B 1F, 6-31-10 Jingu-mae,
Shibuya-ku
03-6419-8136
toga.jp

ALICE AND THE PIRATES
La Foret Harajuku B1, 5F;
1-11-6 Jingu-mae, Shibuya-ku
03-3401-7009
babyssb.co.jp

ORIENTAL BAZAAR
5-9-13 Jingu-mae, Shibuya-ku
03-3400-3933
www.orientalbazaar.co.jp/en

MEIJI JINGU
明治神宮
1-1 Yoyogikamizono-cho, Shibuya-ku
03-3379-5511
www.meijijingu.or.jp/english

JR Harajuku station (top) and Takeshita-dori

BARGAIN HUNTING

100-YEN SHOPS
100円ショップ

DAISO HARAJUKU
Village 107, 1-19-24 Jingu-mae, Shibuya-ku
03-5775-9641
www.daiso-sangyo.co.jp/english

NATURAL KITCHEN SHIBUYA
Shibuya Mark City West Mall 2F, 1-12-1
Dogenzaka, Shibuya-ku
03-3464-7737
www.natural-kitchen.jp

NATURAL KITCHEN SOLAMACHI
Solamachi 1F, Tokyo Skytree Town, 1-1-2
Oshiage, Sumida-ku
03-5610-2746
www.natural-kitchen.jp

Daiso Harajuku

A welcome sight for the budget-conscious traveler is the 100-yen shop, where all items cost only 100 yen. The depth and breadth of the selection, from food to sundries, tableware, cookware, stationery, clothing, and cosmetics, will make your eyes pop. Since the stores keep costs down by buying in bulk, the quality of the goods is generally high. You can often find nearly the same items being sold at supermarkets right next door for two to three times the price. These stores may bear a resemblance to American 99-cent stores, but you're in for a surprise when you see the kinds of things you can get for just 100 yen.

The prototypical Daiso chain of 100-yen shops handles 90,000 items, with 1,000 new ones joining the roster every month. A lot of Japanese people use 100-yen shops to outfit themselves with their daily necessities. You just need to guard against getting reverse sticker shock and picking up things you don't really need or want. There are locations opening in Canada, America, and Australia, and there have been some in Asia for a while already, but here you can find a lot of items unique to Japan. A savvy shopper can pick up some great gifts and souvenirs for only 100 yen.

There are a lot of different shops, but Daiso Harajuku on Takeshita Street has a wide range of items and is located conveniently for travelers. For women in particular, try Natural Kitchen, which sells sundries made of all-natural materials, and stylish lifestyle items. Here you can buy Japanese cookware and kitchen equipment like you'd find at Williams Sonoma for just 100 yen. The Shibuya Mark City location, near the Shibuya station, and the Tokyo Solamachi location, at the Tokyo Skytree Town, are conveniently located for a visit while you're in the area sightseeing.

Hotel ℃

Now there are also convenience stores, such as Lawson 100, where all items are 100 yen. You can eat for a song by stocking up on *nigiri*, sandwiches, drinks, and snacks here (the prices undercut even regular convenience stores).

CAPSULE HOTELS
カプセルホテル

CAPSULE HOTEL SHIBUYA
(men only)
1-19-14 Dogenzaka, Shibuya-ku
03-3464-1777

℃ (Do-c / former HOTEL SIESTA)
1-8-1 Ebisu, Shibuya-ku
03-3449-5255
do-c.jp/en/

The capsule hotel, a convenient place for spending a night, stands alongside karaoke and conveyor-belt sushi on the roster of groundbreaking business ideas conceived in Japan. The centerpieces of the capsule hotel are the long, narrow capsules that you sleep inside, and that look like the inside of a spaceship. It's a facility that's built around simplicity and functionality. The cocoon-like capsules are usually equipped with amenities like a TV, radio, and bedside phone. They may not be well suited to the very tall or the claustrophobic, but if you compare a night in a capsule hotel to one spent sleeping in economy class on an airplane, the capsules aren't so uncomfortable.

The attraction is the low price (around 3500–5000 yen), and consequently the hotels' use is on the rise among foreigners. The amenities have also been evolving in recent years. Capsule Hotel Shibuya, for example, is equipped with a public bath and sauna and a relaxation room outfitted with massage chairs, so you don't have stay shut up in your own capsule. A night's stay in a hotel like this could make for a great story.

東北
TOHOKU

Ichinoseki City near by Hiraizumi in fog

Visiting Tohoku: Hometown of Heart for Japanese People

The mountainous region offers historic temples, natural springs, pristine scenery and some of the most famous vistas in all of Japan—inspiring travelers and poets centuries.

Traveling through Tohoku you can discover not just the history and culture of the area, but the enduring spirit of the Japanese people.This is the place where kingdoms built on the Buddhist kingdom of heaven rose and fell, and where an author and farmer found his own utopia.

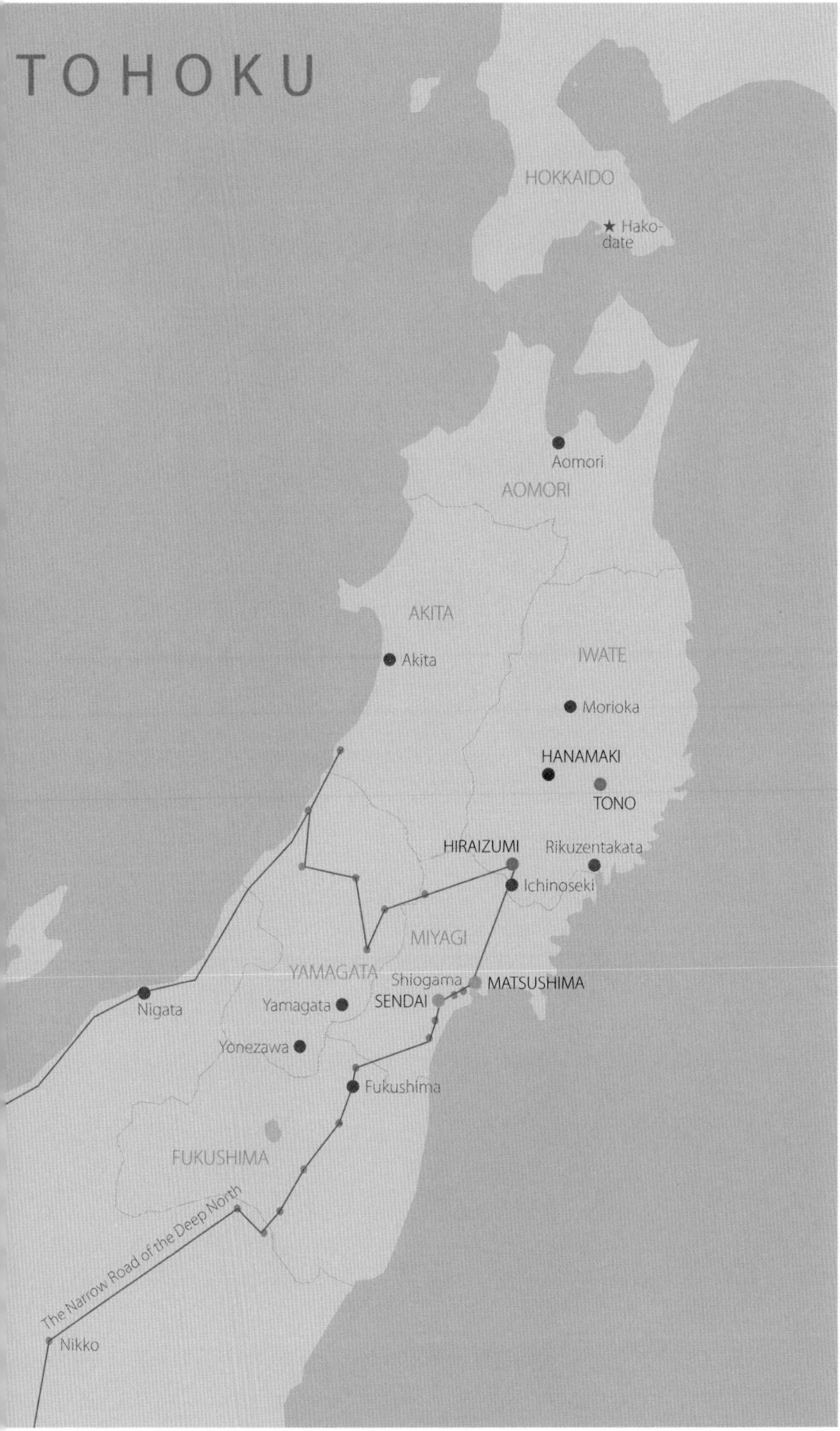

TOHOKU

HOKKAIDO

★ Hako-
date

Aomori

AOMORI

AKITA

IWATE

Akita

Morioka

HANAMAKI

TONO

HIRAIZUMI

Rikuzentakata

Ichinoseki

MIYAGI

YAMAGATA

Shiogama

MATSUSHIMA

Nigata

Yamagata

SENDAI

Yonezawa

Fukushima

FUKUSHIMA

The Narrow Road of the Deep North

Nikko

A dancer performs Hayachine Kagura, a Shinto music and dance

From Tono, the quaint home of the mythical Kappa and the birthplace of Japanese folklore and historic homes that let you experience as life as it once was, to the unparalleled natural scenery that inspired the poet Matsuo Basho to traverse the landscape and write a masterpiece, there is so much to discover in Tohoku. People of all ages are sure to find inspiration in its natural beauty and rich history.

Following the disastrous earthquake and tsunami that devastated the area in 2011, Tohoku became a symbol of Japan's resilience in times of crisis as a poem by native son Miyazawa Kenji captured the nation's spirit and inspired the world. This area, both humble and proud, remains as always "Unbeaten by Rain."

Tohoku, the heart of Japan. Clockwise, from top left: the Tanabata Festival in Sendai; Jodogahama Beach; rice fields; Iwate's Deer Dance; Motsu-ji; Yamaguchi Waterwheel in Tono

仙台/松島
SENDAI/MATSUSHIMA

Full moon on Matsushima

Sendai & Matsushima: Following the Footsteps of Poet Matsuo Basho

You will probably not meet anyone in Japan who has not heard of Matsuo Basho, a haiku poet who lived from 1644 to 1694. He was active in the early part of the Edo period, about 350 years ago. Still now, his great haiku pieces remain deep inside the hearts of the Japanese.

Furuike ya
Kawazu tobikomu
Mizu no oto

Suddenly, a frog jumped into an old pond. The sound broke the silence for the instance, and it went back to the silence again.

Shizukasa ya
Iwani shimiiru
Semino koe

It is so quiet in the dusk and only the cicadas' cries are heard as if they penetrate into the rock.

Time passes by and the look of our world changes, but there are those images of nature and human sentiments that never change over time. Basho's poems vividly depict such invariable essences. Haiku uses only seventeen syllables: five, seven, and five on each line. However, Basho creates a world of images where we can vividly feel the sensations of seeing the ripples made by a frog jumping into a pond or hearing cicada cry on a late summer day.

Basho's haiku show the Japanese philosophy that humans are also part of the greater nature around them. With these views of nature and life, the Japanese have patiently accepted and endured the calamities, such as huge earthquakes and tsunamis, which nature has given. Rather, they have learned the fact that there is no other way but to accept it.

On March 11, 2011, the day of the Tohoku earthquake and tsunami, Nicholas Kristof, who lived in Japan as the head of the *New York Times* Tokyo Bureau and reported on the Kobe Earthquake in 1995, published a column "Sympathy for Japan, and Admiration" on the paper's opinion page. In this piece, he referred to one of Basho's poems to explain the relationship between the Japanese view of nature and their will to reconstruct as follows:

"Americans see themselves as in confrontation with nature, taming it. In contrast, the Japanese conception is that humans are simply one part of nature, riding its tides—including many, many earthquakes throughout history.... In an essay in the *Times* after the Kobe quake, I made some of these same points and ended with a 17th century haiku from one of Japan's greatest poets, Basho:

Ukifushi ya
Takeno-ko to naru
Hito no hate

BASHO AND DATE CLAN

The vicissitudes of life.
Sad, to become finally
A bamboo shoot.

I find something noble and courageous in Japan's
resilience and perseverance, and it will be on display in
the coming days."

It might be incomprehensible that a human becomes
a bamboo shoot. The mere seventeen syllables of this
poem reflect the larger sense of the complexity of the
world, concepts like rising and falling, the hollowness
of life, nature's greatness swallowing everything and
creating new life, reincarnation, and so on.

Haiku's minimalist aesthetic, which aims to capture
a piece of nature within the syllables of five, seven,
and five, deeply relates with the philosophy of Zen
Buddhism. (Zen is an enlightened religious and mental
state attained by striving to achieve spiritual awakening
and serenity of mind.) Steve Jobs, the late founder of
Apple, was also known to have been involved with Zen
philosophy. The beauty of Apple's product designs,
which results in the elimination of waste, seems to
relate to the world of Basho's haiku, which is at once
simple and profound. It becomes more important to
coexist with nature in the 21st century. Basho's Zen-like
philosophy may attract more people's attention.

Basho is often described as a poet who lived on journeys
and died on journeys. The most well known journey that
he took was the one to the northern Tohoku/Hokuriku
region when he was 46 years old. It was at the time that
people said it was long enough to live to 50. It must
have taken courage to depart for a long journey such
as this one at his age. He only was accompanied by
one apprentice named Sora and took paths through
mountains on foot, risking his life. When he left Edo for

WHAT IS A HAIKU? HISTORY & FAMOUS POETS

During the Heian period, the traditional, staid poetic art form underwent a transformation to lighter, airier poems. This new form of poetry, *haikai*, began with a triplet called a *hokku*. Basho, born Matsuo Kinsako, turned the hokku into its own independent poem, the haiku, with three lines made of five, seven, and five syllables, respectively. The haiku's goal was to portray lightness, and to describe a natural, everyday event in the simplest way.

Basho remains one of the most celebrated and read Japanese poets. Other poets that contributed to and helped shaped haiku include Buson, Issa, and Shiki. Together with Basho they are known as "The Great Four."

WHAT IS WABI-SABI?

Wabi-sabi is the aesthetic philosophy of finding beauty in the imperfect, the impermanent, and the incomplete. In home décor, wabi-sabi favors natural elements that have been or will be exposed to aging. In the arts, ikebana, haiku, pottery, and the tea ceremony often exemplify this philosophy of the impermanence and constant flux of all things.

the journey, he said farewell in tears to those who came to see him off. He must have thought he may never see them again.

The travelogue that he wrote on this trip of over a half year, *Oku no Hoshomichi* (The Narrow Road to the Deep North), became his masterpiece. It is surprisingly short, probably due to many revisions and eliminations of unnecessary things. However, the charm of Basho's writing, which often described as *"wabi"* and *"sabi,"* (subtle taste, elegant simplicity, and subdued refinement) is fully expressed in this work.

The opening sentence of this travelogue's preface is all too popular. Dr. Donald Keene, professor emeritus at Columbia University and a leading scholar of Japanese literature, translates it as follows:

"The months and days are the travelers of eternity. The years that come and go are also voyagers."

Although Basho's travelogue can be interpreted in a variety of ways, making it very difficult to translate, it has been translated and published in several versions of English, as well as in French, German, Spanish, Portuguese, Italian, and Russian. In fact, the famous poem introduced in the beginning of this chapter

Basho's departure from Oku no Hosomichi gakan, by Yosa Buson, 1778

"Furuike ya, kawazu tobikomu, mizuno oto" is said to have been translated in foreign languages in over 100 different versions, which shows Basho's literature is highly recognized beyond borders and time.

It is believed that the purpose of the journey of *The Narrow Road of the Deep North* is to visit the sights called *utamakura*, which had been portrayed in the famous poems of all time. In the preface, Basho wrote that he left for the journey in a hurry because he had a strong urge, as if he was possessed by a god of temptation. However, judging from the fact that Sora had done a thorough investigation in advance and made contact to people concerned, it seems like a well-prepared journey.

On his journey, Basho lamented over the changed scenery of the sites once celebrated in the greatest poems, which he had longed to see for so long. On the other hand, he was excited when he found historic sites appearing the same way as he had imagined from those poems. After these experiences, he came to form the artistic theory *fueki ryuko* (permanent values and change). Basho believed that ideal poems and literature needed to contain trends, which change with the time, but also possess eternal truth, which always inspires the human mind regardless of the time.

This philosophy reaches beyond the world of the arts and has implications to business and life in general.

The remains of Sendai Castle

Follow the Footsteps of Basho

Let us now follow the footsteps of Basho to the road of
the deep north. The first stop is Matsushima in Miyagi
Prefecture, which is one of what are called the three most
scenic spots in Japan.

Basho wrote before departing his home in Fukagawa, Edo,
in 1689, "Now I start getting ready for the trip, I cannot stop
thinking of the beautiful moon in Matsushima." He was so
looking forward to visiting this location, which was to be
the highlight of the whole journey.

To get to there, Basho entered Shiogama through Sendai
and traveled to Matsushima on a small boat.

To follow his path, we can go to Sendai first. While Basho
and Sora took over a month to get to Sendai after leaving
Edo and traveled through Nikko and so forth, modern
travelers may prefer to take Tohoku *shinkansen* directly
there in the more impatient 21st century. With the latest

BASHO AND DATE CLAN

train model Hayabusa, which just appeared in 2011, it takes only 1 hour and 36 minutes between Tokyo Station and Sendai Station.

Enya would be a good choice if you want to listen to music while on board. Enya made a song called "Sumiregusa" (from the album *Amarantine*), inspired by the haiku Basho created on his journey at age 42, *"Yamaji kite, naniyara yukasi sumiregusa"* (On a mountain road, heart goes out, to a wild violet.) Basho touched the heart of the Irish siren some 300 years later.

Sendai is where Date family, one of the major clans of *daimyo* (feudal lords) in Edo period, had their castle. When Basho visited Sendai, the Sendai Castle, which was built by the founder of the clan, Date Masamune, was still standing tall on Aoba Mountain overlooking the Hirose River. According to *The Narrow Road to the Deep North*, Basho and Sora stayed four or five nights here.

Unfortunately, the building of Sendai Castle no longer exists. At the site where the castle tower once was, there is the statute of Lord Masamune, courageously mounted on a horse, overlooking the center of Sendai, also called the City of Greenery.

Date Masamune remains one of the most popular samurai lords even today. He is called *Dokugan-ryu* (One-eyed Dragon) due to the fact that he lost the eyesight in his right eye when he was young. He was known for using avant-garde designs for his armor, such as a helmet with a crescent-shaped crest, and for his bold performance. It is

Statue of Date Masamune at the Sendai castle ruins

211

Sunrise at Matsushima

believed that the Japanese started calling a stylish sleek man *Date otoko* (*"otoko"* means man). There is a strong belief that Masamune's war helmet, owned by the Sendai City Museum, became the motif for the mask of Darth Vader in *Star Wars*. They say that the museum actually sent the information about this helmet in response to a request from Hollywood.

Today, nearly 400 years after his death, he has become a popular character as the hero of novels, TV dramas, and games.

About a 30-minute ride on a JR train from Sendai will take you to Matsushima, the scenic treasure Basho longed for. It is also one of the sightseeing spots related to Masamune. If you wish to trace the same route that Basho traveled, take JR Senseki Line to get off at Hon-shiogama Station, where you can take an excursion boat to Matsushima. The Basho cruise runs about 50 minutes, touring in the Matsushima Bay studded with some 260 islands of various sizes. The current pier at Matsushima is believed to be at about the same spot where Basho landed.

When you get off the boat, you will find the approach to the Zuigan-ji Temple, one of the most famous Zen temples in the Tohoku region, right in front of you. On your right,

EXCERPT FROM *THE NARROW ROAD TO THE DEEP NORTH* : MATSUSHIMA

(English translation by Nobuyuki Yuasa)

Much praise has already been lavished on the wonders of the islands of Matsushima. Yet if further praise is possible, I would like to say that here is the most beautiful spot in the whole country of Japan, and that the beauty of these islands is not in the least inferior to the beauty of Lake Dotei or Lake Seiko in China. The islands are situated in a bay about three miles wide in every direction and open to the sea through a narrow mouth on the south-east side. Just as the River Sekko in China is made full at each swell of the tide, so is this bay filled with the brimming water of the ocean and the innumerable islands are scattered over it from one end to the other. Tall islands point to the sky and level ones prostrate themselves before the surges of water. Islands are piled above islands, and islands are joined to islands, so that they look exactly like parents caressing their children or walking with them arm in arm. The pines are of the freshest green and their branches are curved in exquisite lines, bent by the wind constantly blowing through them. Indeed, the beauty of the entire scene can only be compared to the most divinely endowed of feminine countenances, for who else could have created such beauty but the great god of nature himself? My pen strove in vain to equal this superb creation of divine artifice.

Oshima Island where I landed was in reality a peninsula projecting far out into the sea. This was the place where the priest Ungo had once retired, and the rock on which he used to sit for meditation was still there. I noticed a number of tiny cottages scattered among the pine trees and pale blue threads of smoke rising from them. I wondered what kind of people were living in those isolated houses, and was approaching one of them with a strange sense of yearning, when, as if to interrupt me, the moon rose glittering over the darkened sea, completing the full transformation to a night-time scene. I lodged in an inn overlooking the bay, and went to bed in my upstairs room with all the windows open. As I lay there in the midst of the roaring wind and driving clouds, I felt myself to be in a world totally different from the one I was accustomed to. My companion Sora wrote:

Clear voiced cuckoo,
Even you will need
The silver wings of a crane
To span the islands of Matsushima.

I myself tried to fall asleep, suppressing the surge of emotion from within, but my excitement was simply too great.

Oshima Island and Togetsu-kyo bridge

Zuigan-ji Temple and its approach

there is Godaido, the symbol of Matsushima. This temple hall is believed to have been built in 807, but the current building was rebuilt in the early 17th century by Date Masamune. It is the oldest remaining building in Tohoku constructed in the Momoyama style.

While you are on board the boat or on a hill, take a good look at the view of Matsushima Bay. Basho praised the view, comparing it to "a beautiful lady with makeup looking melancholy" ... "impossible to describe with [any] expressions and words." Such views remain unchanged.

The view from Kanrantei is, in particular, highly recommended. This was the Date family's "Moon-Watching Palace," a pavilion to gaze upon the moon during cool evenings. Now it is a historic landmark , where you can have *matcha* green tea and sweets as you overlook the beautiful islands of Matsushima Bay. The inn that Basho stayed at is now a building where you will find souvenir stores and restaurants. You can dine here while gazing at the famous view that Basho once enjoyed. Basho particularly looked forward to viewing Matsushima's "Great Moon." According to locals, the view of moon over the cedar woods by the approach of Zuigan-ji Temple is the most attractive of all.

BASHO AND DATE CLAN

fusuma sliding doors at Zuigan-ji Temple; the site of the inn where Basho stayed

It is interesting that Basho did not write a single poem about Matsushima, which he was so eager to visit. Basho wrote that he was too overwhelmed.

Sora, who accompanied Basho, recorded in his diary that the poet visited Godaido and Oshima Island, a medieval pilgrimage site, and thoroughly observed Zuigan-ji. Zuigan-ji is the family temple of the Date family, which was built in early Heian period. It was very popular during the Kamakura period but lost its prosperity in the Sengoku period. In the Edo period, Masamune took five years to build the current majestic temple. The main building and the Zen kitchen present Momoyama-style architecture, such as the extravagantly painted *fusuma* sliding doors. In *The Narrow Road to the Deep North*, Basho seemed very surprised and impressed with this temple, exclaiming, "gloriously shining with golden walls, it is a stately temple like in the pure land."

Sendai, Shiogama, and Matsushima all suffered major damage by the earthquake and tsunami disasters of March 11, 2011. The damage from the tsunami was especially severe. In Matsushima, sightseeing ferries were washed ashore, and the Togetsu-kyo bridge crossing to Oshima

Sukashi-bashi bridge

Island (where the meditation caves for the monks and Basho's poem monument are located) was also knocked down. However, Matsushima did not face the same level of devastation as other coastal areas and has started a quick recovery. Those many islands scattered inside Matsushima Bay blocked the tsunami waves. Basho must be very relieved in another world.

Sukashi-bashi bridge of Godaido is believed to be a "bridge to bring romance" and, by luck, it did not suffer damage from the recent disaster. Now, it is believed to be even luckier.

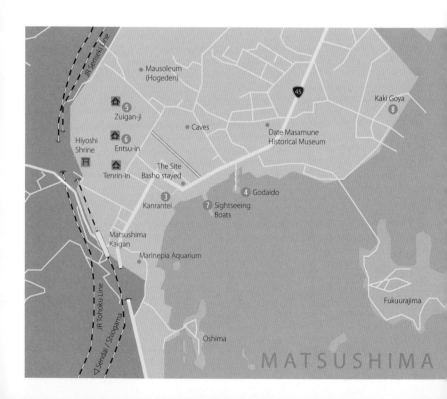

JR Senseki Line

Mausoleum
(Hogeden)

45

Kaki Goya
8

5
Zuigan-ji

Caves

Date Masamune
Historical Museum

Hiyoshi
Shrine

6
Entsu-in

The Site
Basho stayed

Tenrin-in

4 Godaido

3
Kanrantei

7 Sightseeing
Boats

Matsushima
Kaigan

Marinepia Aquarium

Fukuurajima

JR Tohoku Line

◁Sendai / Shiogama

Oshima

MATSUSHIMA

WAS BASHO A NINJA?

Basho's journey of *The Narrow Road to the Deep North* may have had a hidden purpose. Basho was originally from Iga-Ueno (an old name for Iga City, Mie Prefecture), a place known as the hometown of the ninjas. Could Basho have had anything to do with these specially trained spies and mercenaries? Of course, no one suspects the poet actually used the ninja arts like a manga character from *NARUTO*. Instead, he may have been spying for the central government, finding out inside information on the Sendai (Date) Clan.

One of the reasons for this suspicion is the speed of this journey. Calculations based on the diary of Basho's companion Sora showed they sometimes walked as much as 31 mi (50 km) a day. Basho had almost reached the average life expectancy at the time; he died just five years after this journey at 51. How could he have physically done it without the special training?

Moreover, traveling required permission from the government back in the Edo period, and was permitted only for limited numbers of people. However, Basho traveled many times, showing little difficulty either financially or legally. Therefore, it is suspected that the government supplied the money and travel permits on the condition that he spy for them.

At the time, there was tension between Tokugawa government and Sendai (Date) Clan. But Basho's well-known status as a poet allowed him to enter Sendai and visit important places freely for the purpose of creative activities. Among these sites was the Date family's Zuigan-ji Temple, a possible fortified castle with a solid structure that faced the ocean in the front and a mountain in the back. Basho checked up on it thoroughly, supporting the suspicion that he may have been acting as a spy. Also, it makes some wonder why Basho did not create any poems while he was in Matsushima. Was he was too busy committing espionage? Was the masterpiece *The Narrow Road to the Deep North* actually a cover for spying? Following in Basho's footsteps you can explores these mysteries through time.

WHERE TO SEE

Sendai Castle Site and Sendai city

Sightseeing information on Sendai:
www.sentabi.jp/en

Sightseeing information on Matsushima:
Matsushima Tourism Association web site
www.matsushima-kanko.com/en

From Sendai Station, use Sendai-city's
sightseeing bus, called Loople Sendai, or
a taxi.

Loople Sendai

①ZUIHODEN
瑞鳳殿

Loople Stop #4
23-2 Otamayashita, Aoba-ku, Sendai
022-262-6250
www.zuihoden.com/english/english.
htm

The mausoleum of Date Masamune
is surrounded by 370-year-old cedar
woods. It was burned down during
the war in 1945 but was rebuilt in
1979. It was remodeled again in 2001,
fully recreating and the gorgeous
Momoyama-style building. Masamune,
together with the second and third lords
of the Date clan, is entombed here.

❷ SENDAI CASTLE SITE
仙台城跡

Loople Stop #5 (Aoba Castle Museum)
or #6 (Aoba Castle Ruins)
1 Kawauchi, Aoba-ku, Sendai
022-214-8259
www.sentabi.jp/en/tourist/
sendaijouato.html

The castle where the lord of Sendai, Date Masamune, lived was built in 1602. Since it was built on the natural stronghold of Aoba Mountain, it was called Aoba Castle. Today, only part of the stone walls and the Otemon Waki-yagura, recreated in 1967, are remaining. However, you can have a panoramic view of Sendai City from the castle tower, which is a popular place to view the city at night. The Aoba Castle Museum is located inside the castle site; there you can see the original castle recreated by computer graphics.

Go back to Sendai Station and take JR Senseki Line to Matsushima Kaigan Station. You can travel on foot around Matsushima.

Zuihoden

Godaido

WHAT ARE "JAPAN'S THREE GREAT VIEWS?"

Matsushima, Amanohashidate (Kyoto) and Miyajima (a World Heritage site in Hiroshima) are often referred to as "Japan's Three Great Views." It is believed that, in the early Edo period, a Confucianist named Hayashi Shunsai walked across the nation and selected these three sites for their most spectacular views. The ocean blue and green pine trees create a striking contrast that moves people's hearts in each location. These three views have appeared in many poems and literature, and it can be said that they are the origin of the Japanese love for traveling. *Michelin Green Guide Japan*, first published in 2009, awarded three stars each to Matsushima and Miyajima, while no mention was given to Amanohashidate. In the Matsushima area, Zuigan-ji received three stars, and Entsu-in and Sankeiden received two stars. You will see more French tourists here recently thanks to the Michelin guide.

SENDAI

Kanrantei

Godaido

❸ KANRANTEI
観瀾亭

56 Aza-chonai, Matsushima,
Matsushima-machi, Miyagi
022-353-3355

Sendai clan lords used this palace
for a summertime retreat and moon
viewing during the Edo period. It was
originally part of Fushimi Momoyama
Castle, which was built by Toyotomi
Hideyoshi, the daimyo who unified
Japan. Hideyoshi gave it to Masamune
and Masamune's successor Tadamune
is said to have rebuilt it at this location.
Gozanoma, a living room for serving
guests, is furnished with brightly painted
sliding doors with gold leaf. Here you
can enjoy matcha green tea and sweets
while looking out over Matsushima Bay.

❹ GODAIDO
五大堂

A symbol of Matsushima, this small
Buddhist worship hall stands as it was
400 years ago. The bridge to the temple
is called Sukashi-bashi (see-through
bridge) because you can see the ocean
below your feet between its floorboards.

❺ ZUIGAN-JI TEMPLE
瑞巌寺

91 Aza-chonai, Matsushima,
Matsushima-machi, Miyagi
022-354-2023
www.zuiganji.or.jp

This Zen temple was originally built
during the Heian period, and was
rebuilt by Date Masamune in 1609. It
is currently under a major renovation
until the spring of 2018 and the main
hall (a national treasure) is off limits.
However, the other buildings, such as
the mausoleum for Masamune's wife,
Megohime, are open to public in the
meantime. The ruins of caves, carved
by ascetic monks about 700 years ago
during the Kamakura period, stand
alongside the approach to the temple.

At Zuigan-ji, you will find wooden
daruma dolls with written oracles inside
for sale. These round figures encourage
completion of a goal. When you buy the
doll, both eyes are blank, fill one in when
you set the goal and the other when you
complete it.

The Kannon statue at the ruins of the caves in Zuigan-ji

MATSUSHIMA

221

❻ ENTSU-IN TEMPLE
円通院

67 Aza Chonai Matsushima
Matsushima-machi, Miyagi
022-354-3206

Located near Zuigan-ji, Entsu-in temple houses the mausoleum of Date Masamune's grandson, Mitsumune. The mausoleum is called Sankeiden. The gardens are especially elegant. There is a rose garden, which is rare for Buddhist temples, and so Entsu-in is also called the "Rose Temple." Here you can visit the popular matchmaker god Enmusubi Kannon and try to make your own *juzu*, a Buddhist rosary, for avoiding bad luck. This temple is lit up fantastically during the fall foliage season.

Sankeiden at Entsu-in

THE STORY OF ENTSU-IN TEMPLE AND ITS ROSES

Entsu-in Temple was built in 1646 in order to house the mausoleum of Date Masamune's grandson, Mitsumune. Mitsumune excelled in both literary and military arts, and there were high expectations for his future. However, he died of a disease at age 19 while he was in Edo Castle. There is a rumor that the Tokugawa Clan, fearing his talent, poisoned the boy. Date Tadamune, the successor of Masamune, built a mausoleum, Sankeiden, for his beloved son, Mitsumune, and enshrined a statute of him riding on a white horse.

The portable shrine is painted with Western-style roses, the symbol of Rome, and daffodils, the symbol of Florence, which Hasekura Tsunenaga brought back from his trip to Italy and Spain as a delegate of Masamune between 1613 and 1620. Other Western motifs include hearts and spades. During the Edo period, the use of such Western motifs for décor was unheard of in Japan. The ruling Tokugawa Clan had issued the Anti-Christian Edicts right after Masamune sent his delegate to Europe and began cracking down on the Christians, and closed the nation's door to the outside world. Because of this, this mausoleum's door was kept closed for 350 years and no one was supposed to see inside.

Masamune had sent his delegate to Europe because he wanted to get permission from the king of Spain to trade with Mexico, and to request that the Pope send missionaries to Sendai and promote Christianity in his territory. The Date family had no choice but to give up this original idea and follow the Tokugawa's policy changes. Their frustration is easy to imagine. The fact that they built such a mausoleum decorated with Western cultural influences at the time of Japan's isolationist policy may give you a glimpse of the Date family's sense of pride. Now you can see why Date Masamune is called the great man who Tokugawa Ieyasu feared most.

MATSUSHIMA

The statue of Mitsumune in Sankeiden

❼ SIGHTSEEING BOATS
遊覧船

Nio-Iwa

Shima-meguri Nioh-maru Course departs from Matsushima Pier.
For Information:
Matsuhima Shima-meguri Kankosen
022-354-2233

Basho Cruise (The Narrow Road to the Deep North Course) travels along the same route that Basho took. It runs between Matsushima and Shiogama, departing from either side.
For Information:
Marubun Matsushima Kisen
022-365-3611
www.marubun-kisen.com/english/matsushima/basho.html

A sightseeing boat trip cruising in the Matsushima Bay is an experience not to be missed. The ride lasts about 50 minutes, as you feel the mild ocean breeze and enjoy this famous scenic site, one of the so-called "Japan's Three Great Views." The boats cruise around the bay between the 260 islands of various sizes and shapes, including Futago-jima, Kabuto-jima, Kane-jima, and Nioh-jima. English narration is broadcast during the cruise. They also sell food onboard for the seagulls, which follow the boats around waiting for a treat.

Kaki-Goya

OYSTERS
牡蠣

8 Kaki Goya
12-1 Matsushima Higashihama,
Matsushima-machi, Miyagi
022-354-2618

Matsushima is famous for oysters. You can see many oyster farming rafts floating on Matsushima Bay. If the sight makes you hungry, you can eat deep-fried oysters, bowls of rice topped with oysters, oyster pot with miso, and other oyster dishes in many restaurants here. There are even novelty menu items like oyster curry buns and oyster burgers, which you will not find anywhere else. Oyster season lasts between October and March. There are oyster specialty restaurants, which open only during the season. The most popular one is Kaki Goya (oyster hut). This restaurant is run by the local tourism association.

They offer all-you-can-eat shell-baked oysters right out of the ocean (45-minute time limit), which always draws a line waiting to get in. There is a more pricy one-hour all-you-can-eat option for which you can make a reservation.

Also note that Shiogama is one of the largest tuna fishing ports in Japan and there are many sushi restaurants. Some tourists come here just for good sushi.

MATSUSHIMA

Clockwise, from top right: oysters at Kaki-Goya; Shiogama port with tuna; sashimi at Sushi Shirahata in Shiogama

225

平泉
HIRAIZUMI

Ōi-do (Konjikido) at Chuson-ji

Hiraizumi: The Tragedy of the Oshu Fujiwara Family

On the journey of *The Narrow Road of the Deep North*, one of the places Basho was particularly eager to visit was Hiraizumi.

Before tracing Basho's path, we should look back at the history of Hiraizumi. It is impossible to fully appreciate *The Narrow Road of the Deep North* without knowing of the rise and fall of the people of this place, which was once a golden paradise made by the wealth of gold dust.

The area around Hiraizumi was registered in 2011 as a UNESCO World Heritage Site for its temples, gardens, and archaeological sites representing the Buddhist pure land. The news gave bright hope for recovery to the Tohoku region and to the entire country of Japan after suffering from the huge earthquake, tsunami, and nuclear disasters of March 2011. It is rather meaningful that the concept of pure land was recognized worldwide in the very year that this region suffered an unprecedented disaster.

Fuhiwara Kiyohira   Motohira   Hidehira

What is the "Buddhist pure land" that people strived to achieve in Hiraizumi? A Buddhist pure land is a celestial realm of peace where people would live in equality. In Hiraizumi, people hoped to create a pure land as they were living, rather than as a destination to go after death.

It was the Oshu (now called Tohoku or Northeast Japan) Fujiwara family who governed this region for around 100 years from the beginning of the 12th century and carried out this dream. The founder of the Oshu Fujiwara family, Kiyohira, tried to hold a memorial service for every life lost, friend and foe alike, in order to resolve the memories of the bloody battles over the ruling power in the late 11th century. Starting with the erection of Chuson-ji Temple, he endeavored to put Buddhism at the center of governance, and to create an ideal city at Hiraizumi that would be rich and peaceful, an earthly representation of a pure land.

Kiyohira's vision was passed on to Motohira, the second generation, and Hidehira, the third generation of the Oshu Fujiwara family. Using the wealth gained from the gold dust panned in the region, they achieved a cultural center in rural Tohoku that rivaled Kyoto, the capital of the nation at the time.

They aimed to create a peaceful world where people with hearts like Buddha lived. It might seem a miracle that such idealistic government lasted as long as 100 years.

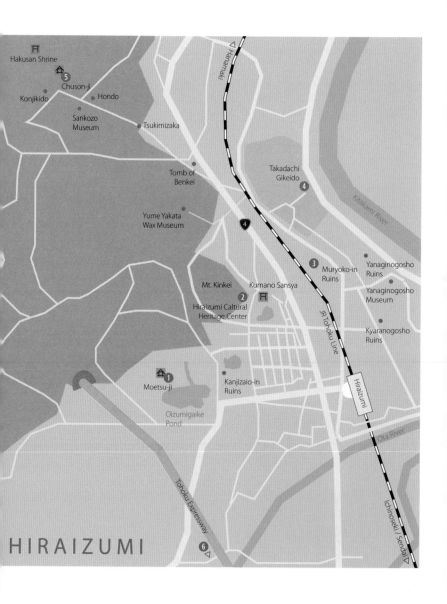

Hakusan Shrine

5 Chuson-ji

Konjikido   Hondo

Sankozo
Museum   Tsukimizaka

Tomb of
Benkei

Takadachi
Gikeido
4

Yume Yakata
Wax Museum

4

3 Muryoko-in
Ruins

Yanaginogosho
Ruins

Mt. Kinkei   Kumano Sansya

2
Hiraizumi Cultural
Heritage Center

Yanaginogosho
Museum

Kyaranogosho
Ruins

Kitakami River

JR Tohoku Line

Hiraizumi

Moetsu-ji
1

Kanjizaio-in
Ruins

Oizumigaike
Pond

Ota River

HIRAIZUMI

Tohoku Expressway

6

Ichinoseki Sendai

Hanamaki

TIMELESS HERO: MINAMOTO YOSHITSUNE

Minamoto Yoshitsune is still a very popular tragic hero more than 800 years after his death. Known as Ushiwaka-maru as a child, he was a military genius and a war hero during the Minamoto clan's punitive expedition against the Taira clan. However, he ended his own life at the age 31 in tragedy.

His story raised the compassion of people; therefore, myths were added to his story over time. One of the most influential stories about Yoshitsune was *Gikeiki*, a war tale written in the Muromachi period after about 200 years after his death. This story formed the image of the hero Yoshitsune, which inspired many literary and art works, including noh and *kabuki* plays, *bunraku* (Japanese puppet theater), movies, novels, and games.

One of the most popular legends of Yoshitsune is about the dramatic encounter with the warrior monk Benkei, who would become his faithful follower, at the bridge of Gojo in Kyoto. The scene where the small Ushiwaka-maru (Yoshitsune), tumbled down the giant Benkei became the subject of a Japanese school song. Benkei is said to have died in the last battle at Hiraizumi, standing at the entrance to Yoshitsune's quarter, receiving a barrage of flying arrows from the enemy forces in order to save his master. The legends spread by *Gikeiki* and are regarded as historical fact today. In the legends, Yoshitsune is described as a handsome young prince. Thus, popular idols or handsome actors usually play his roles in TV dramas and movies.

There is a persistent legend about Yoshitsune's immortality. In fact, he is still alive on stage. Starting from the Edo period, Yoshitsune has been such a popular theme in *noh* and *kabuki* plays that there is an entire genre called *Gikei-mono* (Yoshitsune-themed plays). One of the most popular plays is *Kanjincho* (The Subscription List), where Benkei protects Yoshitsune and his followers using his wisdom and herculean strength on the way to Oshu as they flee from Yoshitsune's older brother Yoritomo, which generations of top *kabuki* actors have played. *Yoshitsune Senbon-zakura* (Yoshitsune and the Thousand Cherry Trees) is also famous of this kind.

Minamoto Yoshitsune

BASHO AND BUDDIST PURE LAND

Fujiwara Festival at Hiraizumi in May

Unfortunately, however, the prosperity of the Oshu Fujiwara family came to end in 1189.

The key figure in the family's decline was Minamoto Yoshitsune, who was staying in Hiraizumi during the time of the third lord, Hidehira. Yoshitsune's older brother was Yoritomo, who would later establish the Kamakura shogunate. At the time, Yoritomo was expanding his power, and had gained control of the western part of Japan. Yoshitsune helped Yoritomo and won many battles against the Taira clan. However, Yoritomo began to disfavor Yoshitsune because of his talent and finally ousted him from his army.

Yoshitsune fled to Hiraizumi, where Hidehira offered him protection. When Hidehira died, his son, Yasuhira, took over the family and Yoritomo ordered him to eliminate Yoshitsune. Yasuhira went against Hidehira's will and attacked Yoshitsune, forcing him to take his own life with his wife and children at his castle in Takadachi. He was only 31 years old.

Despite Yasuhira's act of allegiance, Yoritomo later attacked Yasuhira and gained control of Hiraizumi. His large army marched into the city and burnt down

Kitakami River from Takadachi

many temples. The Kamakura shogunate protected Hiraizumi after the new order was established, but it was never the same golden city that was once compared to Kyoto and Nara.

Basho visited Hiraizumi 500 years after the downfall of the Oshu Fujiwara family. What had once been magnificent mansions had turned into a grass field, with no sign of its former prosperity. Basho was overwhelmed with a flood of emotions and cried, standing on Takadachi, the hill where Yoshitsune lived and ended his life.

Natsu-kusa ya
Tsuwamono domo ga
Yume no ato

Now it is just a field covered with summer grass but it was here where heroes sacrificed their lives for their dreams.

It is one of the most famous poems in Japan, written by Basho, remembering Yoshitsune's destiny and his loyal retainers who followed him to the end. Knowing this history, when you walk up to Takadachi you may feel the same reverence as Basho.

BASHO AND BUDDIST PURE LAND

EXCERPT FROM *THE NARROW ROAD TO THE DEEP NORTH*:

HIRAIZUMI (English translation by Nobuyuki Yuasa)

It is here that the glory of the three generations of the Fujiwara family passed away like a snatch of empty dream. The ruins of the main gate greeted my eyes a mile before I came upon Lord Hidehira's mansion, which had been utterly reduced to rice-paddies. Mount Kinkei along retained its original shape. As I climbed one of the foothills called Takadate, where Lord Yoshitsune met his death, I saw the Kitakami River running though the plains of Nambu in its full force, and its tributary, Koromogawa, winding along the site of the Izumi-ga-shiro castle and pouring into the big river directly below my eyes. The ruined house of Lord Yasuhira was located to the north of the barrier-gate of Koromo-ga-seki, thus blocking the entrance from the Nambu area and forming a protection against barbarous intruders from the north. Indeed, many a feat of chivalrous valour was repeated here during the short span of the three generations, but both the actors and the deeds have long been dead and passed into oblivion. When a country is defeated, there remain only mountains and rivers, and on a ruined castle in spring only grasses thrive. I sat down on my hat and wept bitterly till I almost forgot time.

A thicket of summer grass
Is all that remains
Of the dreams and ambitions
Of ancient warriors.

I caught a glimpse
Of the frost hair of Kanefusa
Wavering among
The white blossoms of unohana.
*　　　—Written by Sora*

The interiors of the two sacred buildings of whose wonders I had often heard with astonishment were at least revealed to me. In the library of *sutras* were placed the statues of three nobles who governed this area, and enshrined in the so-called Gold Chapel were the coffins containing their bodies, and three sacred images. These buildings, too, would have perished under the all-devouring grass, their treasures scattered, their jeweled doors broken and their gold pillars crushed, but thanks to the outer frame and a covering of tiles added for protection, they had to survived to be a monument of at least a thousand years.

Even the long rain of May
Has left it untouched —
This Gold Chapel
Aglow in the somber shade.

Statue of Basho at Chuson-ji

Basho's Travels in Hiraizumi

It takes about 10 minutes to walk from JR Hiraizumi station to Takadachi. It is a low-lying hill about 70 meters above sea level, but its panorama is the best one in the Hiraizumi area. You can see the Kitakami River flow slowly below your eyes and Mount Tabashine spreading its mild ridges over green fields. It is such a gentle scene that you may not imagine there was a prosperous city here 900 years ago.

What Basho saw here may not have been much different from what we see today. While human history keeps changing, nature remains the same.

Basho took a phrase from a poem by Du Fu, a famous Chinese poet of the 8th century, to express his deep sentiment at the fact that the river and mountain still remain the same while a city was destroyed: "The country is destroyed; yet mountains and rivers remain and spring comes to the castle; the grass is green again."

At the peak of Takadachi, there is a memorial hall dedicated to Yoshitsune called Gikeido, built by the fourth Sendai Clan lord, Date Tsunamura in 1683. There is a brightly colored wooden sculpture of Yoshitsune in

Gikeido and statue of Yoshitsune

BASHO AND BUDDIST PURE LAND

Statue of Benkei at Benkeido in Chuson-ji

armor inside. It was built five years before Basho visited Hiraizumi, but it is not known whether he stopped by this memorial.

You can find a monument engraved with Basho's poem about summer grass near here.

Next, Basho visited Chuson-ji Temple, the main temple of Tendai sect in the Tohoku region, built in the 9th century. Kiyohira erected a large edifice here in his attempt to create a pure land in Hiraizumi. However, without the support of the Oshu Fujiwara family, the temple buildings had mostly burned down by the 14th century. Basho must have seen the run-down remains of these temples when he visited here. However, the Konjikido (Golden Hall) was miraculously maintained for 900 years through today, and over 3,000 national treasures and other important cultural properties are still stored here.

The main approach to the temple, called Tsukimi-zaka (moon viewing slope), is lined with cedar trees that are 300 to 400 years old and it has a sublime atmosphere.

Tsukimi-zaka

These trees were planted by the Sendai Clan around the time Basho visited here. As you walk up the steep approach, feeling the history around you, you will find Benkeido to your left, which enshrines Yoshitsune's retainer, Benkei. The wooden statute of Benkei guarding Yoshitsune with his own body as he was hit by many arrows is a must see. The tragedy of the price Yoshitsune and the warrior monk Benkei is widely popular among the Japanese; it has become the theme of many stories and *kabuki* plays.

The temple buildings are mostly from the Edo period, built by Sendai Clan. The Main Hall was rebuilt in the 20th century.

The Konjikido (Golden Hall) is further inside. It is the only building that remains from the Oshu Fujiwara period. It is apparent that people wanted to protect this treasure at any cost. In the Kamakura period, the Konjikido was covered by the Oi-do (covering hall) and managed to survive until today.

This magnificent golden structure took Kiyohira as long as 16 years to build. Not only the Buddhist statutes, but its doors, walls, and floors are all covered with gold leaf. As you approach, the golden glow is overwhelming,

Konjikido

representing an earthly image of a pure land paradise. The interior is decorated with the best Buddhist art techniques from the Heian period, including *raden* (mother-of-pearl inlay) design and *makie* (gold or silver lacquer).

The remains of the first three lords of Fujiwara, including Kiyohira, are placed here, along with the statues of three Buddhas.

Konjikido was completed in 1124, a few years before Kiyohira died. He must have been very pleased to see it finished while he was still alive. He died at the age of 73, which was pretty old back in those days.

Konjikido went through a major six-year restoration during the 1960s, which brought the original brilliance back to this golden hall. The Oi-do, which covers and protects Konjikido, was rebuilt in reinforced concrete, taking all possible measures against flame and humidity.

At the time of Basho's visit, the gold leaf was badly damaged and Konjikido had lost its luster. Basho wrote, "the *cloisonné* enamel is discolored, the doors decorated with gems are beaten by the weather, and the pillars with golden leaf are damaged by frost and snow."

Even now, you can spot some damage to the interior, like gold leaf peeling off or discoloration. Upon seeing such sights Basho must have felt pity remembering the rise and fall of the Oshu Fujiwara family.

Basho composed a famous haiku here, which you can see on a monument near the Konjikido.

Samidare no
Furinokoshite ya
Hikarido.

When you go further in inside Chuson-ji, you will see the Kyodo, the wooden Sutra Repository that once housed a national treasure, the *Chusonji-kyo* (Buddhist sutras, or scriptures, written in silver and gold ink on navy blue paper), and former Oi-do, which Basho saw when he visited, as well as a statute of Basho and the monument to *The Narrow Road of the Deep North*.

Since the Golden Hall is a national treasure and very well known, it attracts many visitors. They are fascinated with the beautiful golden interior; many need to pause to catch their breath amid its splendor. Unfortunately though, only few know about the Oshu Fujiwara family's philosophy of building an ideal society to realize the

Basho's haiku monument and Kyodo at Chuson-ji

BASHO AND BUDDIST PURE LAND

View of Yakiishi-dake mountains from Chuson-ji

image of a pure land on earth. Perhaps, most visitors would assume that Oshu Fujiwara built the Konjikido to show off their wealth and power, or that they built it to ensure their own salvation.

Many visitors come in large tour buses directly to the Konjikido, rush into the building as if they came to a theme park, and they do not see any other buildings here. Some of them complain, "It was smaller than expected." That is a wasteful way to visit here. To get better experience, you should walk up the approach, Tsukimi-zaka, to bathe in the clean air and clear your mind before visiting the temples. You should not forget that the Konjikido is also the mausoleum for Fujiwara family.

Konjikido's interior was been decorated with materials that came from overseas, such as great green turban snail shells from tropical oceans for design in mother-of-pearl inlay, red sandalwood, and African ivory. In short, Kiyohira meant to create a pure land with materials from around the world.

CGI rendering of Muryoko-in in the time of the Oshu Fujiwara family

Oshu, now the Tohoku region, was in fact an important trading center at the time of the Oshu Fujiwara family. Moreover, it was Kiyohira's roots that gave him the broad image of a pure land for everyone in the world. Kiyohira was not a scion of any aristocrat or warrior family in Kyoto. He came into power after being forced to experience family quarrels, and had survived a number of wars where he saw many lives lost. His father had the blood of a ruling aristocrat, but his mother was from a regional clan in Tohoku. Kiyohira would call himself "the leader of minorities." This perspective might have been why he sought the most beautiful elements from different cultures.

Kiyohira wanted to build a borderless pure land not limited for humans, but also for all living things. He wished that the Konjikido's golden glory would brighten up the entire world. That might be the reason why only Konjikido was kept intact for 900 years.

According to *The Narrow Road to the Deep North,* Basho did not take in many sights while he was in Hiraizumi.

BASHO AND BUDDIST PURE LAND

Muryoko-in site now

Even though he was looking forward to visiting, he merely stayed for a couple of hours and hurried to the nearby town of Ichinoseki where he stayed the night. Could it be that all he needed was to experience the deep sense of the mortal world on the hill of Takadachi?

"What's left after Hidehira's mansion is farmlands," he wrote. Today, that might be the place marked as the Kyara-no-gosho site. Although Basho did not mention it, he might have passed in front of the original site of Muryoko-in. It was the large building, erected by the third lord Hidehira, following the example of winged Ho-o-do (Phoenix Hall) of Byodo-in in Uji, Kyoto. You will find no building here any more, just a feeling of stillness.

Motsu-ji Temple is also a must-see spot in Hiraizumi, and like Chuson-ji Temple, it is listed by UNESCO as an important part of the world heritage. Basho does not seem to have visited here. Motsu-ji was originally built in 850 and was rebuilt by the second lord Motohira in the 12th century. At the time of the third lord Hidehira, there were 40 temple buildings and 500 monks' quarters. All of the buildings were destroyed by fires later on. All that remains is a beautiful pure land garden with Oizumi-ga-ike pond, and foundation of the original buildings.

Motsu-ji's garden represents a pure world of the Buddha. The temple stands with the mountains as background and the pond, which represents the ocean. The design was created using the philosophy and techniques from *Sakutei-ki*, Japan's oldest garden-making book, written during the Heian period.

It is enjoyable to imagine the glorious temple buildings that were once here while you observe the garden surrounded with the seasonal flowers like irises and bush clovers. The air is smooth and the slight sound of water is refreshing. As you gaze over the mirror-like blue pond, your mind may be purified and regain peace.

Here, you may find your own pure land.

Motsu-ji

BASHO AND BUDDIST PURE LAND

THE JAPANESE-STYLE PURE LAND GARDEN AND *YARIMIZU*

The pure land garden at Motsu-ji Temple is an example of a Japanese-style garden, a gardening concept brought with Buddhism from the Asian mainland, blended with the Japanese indigenous religious faith, Shinto, and developed into an original Japanese technique. For example, Buddhism was brought from India, but Motsu-ji's pond is round as opposed to an Indian garden's square ponds. This round pond became the model that later spread throughout Japan.

The *yarimizu* is a small canal built to draw water from mountain streams to the garden pond. It is believed to be based on *feng shui* principles from China. The present structure was reconstructed using the model of the remains from the Heian period, discovered in 1983. This elegant conduit has cobbled stones on the bottom and the water winds slowly as if it is a river running through a plain. According to the temple's spokesman, mountain water used to be drawn from the west. After the reconstruction, the water came in from the northeast—and miraculously the water of the pond became free from dirt and stagnation.

Gokusui no En (Party of the Winding Stream) is celebrated on the fourth Sunday of May every year when participants float sake cups in the stream and compose *waka* poems. They recreate the image of the elegant Heian period by wearing the traditional kimono, such as *juni-hitoe* (twelve-layered kimonos).

If you visit Hiraizumi at this time of the year, it is worth stopping by.

Gokusui no En

Hiraizmi Tourism Information:
Hiraizumi Tourism Association
hiraizumi.or.jp/en/sightseeing/

❶ MOTSU-JI TEMPLE—
UNESCO WORLD HERITAGE SITE
毛越寺

58 Osawa, Hiraizumi, Iwate
0191-46-2331
www.motsuji.or.jp/english

The elegant pure land garden in this temple is a great place for a stroll. Although the original buildings no longer remain, Jogyodo Hall was rebuilt in the 18th century and has a nice atmosphere. A hidden Buddha here is only shown once every 33 years. The temple holds Ennen-no-mai longevity rites where dances and songs from medieval times are offered to the deities and the Buddha. There is an old haiku monument to "Natsukusa ya…" in Basho's own handwriting. The adjacent garden, Kanjizaio-in, is all that remains of the temple that the second lord Motohira's wife built after his death.

❷ HIRAIZUMI CULTURAL HERITAGE CENTER
平泉文化遺産センター

44 Hanadate, Hiraizumi, Iwate
0191-46-4012
hiraizumi.or.jp/en/sightseeing/
bunkaisan_center/index.html

This is a tourist's center with information on the history of the Oshu Fujiwara family and Hiraizumi's cultural heritage. It offers a good introduction to the area. Free admission.

BASHO AND BUDDIST PURE LAND

❸ MURYOKO-IN RUINS—
UNESCO WORLD HERITAGE SITE
無量光院跡

Aza Hanatate Chinai, Hiraizumi, Iwate
hiraizumi.or.jp/en/heritage/index.html

Muryoko-in, built by the third lord Hidehira, came close to surpassing the scale of the Byodo-in Ho-o-do (UNESCO World Heritage Site) in Uji, Kyoto, which Muryoko-in was modeled after. The excavated remains, including the foundation stones and the lake's remains, reveal the entire layout where once a bridge, island, a second bridge, and Amida Buddha statute in the main hall all stood in a single line to the west, overlooking Kinkei-san Mountain ahead. During the equinoctial weeks both in spring and fall, the sun would set on the peak of Kinkei-san Mountain behind the main hall. This would make the Amida Buddha statute glow in the setting sun, emitting a halo around the Buddha.

❹ TAKADACHI GIKEIDO
高館 義経堂

14 Yanaginogosho, Hiraizumi, Iwate
0191-46-3300

Takadachi hill is where Minamoto Yoshitsune ended his life. Gikeido Hall stands on the top of the hill to honor him. Basho composed the famous haiku

ENGLISH HAIKU MONUMENT AT MOTSU-JI TEMPLE

There are three haiku monuments to "Natsukusa ya…" in Motsu-ji temple. One is quite old and engraved in Basho's own writing. There is another monument next to it, which is a copy of the original. There is also an English translation monument, translated and brush-written by Nitobe Inazo, and built in 1967. It reads: "The summer grass/ 'Tis all that's left/ Of ancient warriors' dreams."

Nitobe was an educator from Iwate Prefecture. He hoped to serve as a bridge across the Pacific Ocean and contribute to world peace. His book *Bushido: The Soul of Japan* has been widely read around the world.

HIRAIZUMI

PREMISE FOR THE LAND OF GOLD, JIPANGU

Marco Polo's *Books of the Marvels of the World* (The Travels of Marco Polo) is known to have had an immense impact during the Age of Exploration. In this book, Japan was called "the land of gold: Zipangu" where palaces and houses were made with gold. It is believed that these passages were written in China upon hearing rumors about the ornate Chuson-ji Konjiki-do (Golden Hall). Although it created a misunderstanding, Konjiki-do's reputation had spread overseas to China.

CHUSON-JI'S MIRACULOUS LOTUS FLOWERS

In 1950, about 80 lotus seeds were found in the coffin containing the head of the fourth lord Yasuhira. In 1998, the lotus seeds were miraculously revived, and they flowered after 800 years. Since then, the ancient pale pink lotus blossoms flowers in the pond at Chuson-ji Temple every year. This lotus is also called Yasuhira lotus.

"Natsukusa ya…" when he visited here. Sora's haiku "Unohana ni, Kanefusa miyuru, Shiraga kana" describes Kanefusa, who was the elderly attendant for Yoshitsune's wife.

❺ CHUSON-JI TEMPLE—
UNESCO WORLD HERITAGE SITE
中尊寺

202 Koromonoseki, Hiraizumi, Iwate
0191-46-2211
www.chusonji.or.jp

The symbol of Hiraizumi and a UNESCO World Heritage Site, Chuson-ji was built by Kiyohira in the late 11th century. Though some of its splendor has been lost to the years, the elaborately decorated Konjikido Golden Hall remains a stunning monument to the Fujiwara family. The museum, Sankozo, contains more than 3,000 treasures, including the Chuson-ji Sutras.

BASHO AND BUDDIST PURE LAND

❻ GENBIKEI
厳美渓

Kakkoya
211 Takinoue, Genbi-cho
Ichinosek, Iwate
0191-29-2031

Genbikei is one of the famous gorges in the area, and it offers varied natural beauty for visitors to enjoy, including glorious views of the Iwai River that runs through it. It is recommended to visit if you stay in Ichinoseki, following Basho's steps. Genbikei is 20 minutes by bus from Ichinoseki Station. The local specialty is "Flying Rice Dumpling" sold at Kakkoya.

GENBIKEI'S SPECIALTY: KAKKO DANGO

The *dango* (sticky rice dumpling) eatery Kakkoya has been in business for about 100 years. This region is known to produce high quality rice. The shop got this name because the owner, a cheerful old man, was good at mimicking *kakko* (cuckoo). The attraction is the "flying rice dumpling" performance where the rice dumplings are delivered across the gorge. The rice dumplings and tea are put in a basket and carried down on a rope from the shop on the top of the gorge to the customers by the river. They put the national flags on the basket and play the national anthem for the customers from overseas. They offer about 30 national flags.

Three sticks of freshly made dumplings with such a fun performance cost only 400 yen. It is also entertaining to eat by the river listening to the sound of the stream. The sweet taste of the dumplings and the merry characteristics of the shop owner have been passed on for generations. The wooden statute of the founder greets customers today. Be aware that the dumplings are usually sold out by around 4 p.m. The shop is closed from November to February.

HIRAIZUMI

BASHO'S FAMOUS HAIKU

Yamaji kite
Naniyara yukashi
Sumire-kusa

While walking along a mountain road, I just looked aside and found little violet flowers. The humble appearance touched my heart.

Shizukasa-ya
Iwani shimiiru
Semino koe

It is so quiet in the dusk and only the cicadas' cries are heard as if they penetrate into the rock. This haiku was written at Tateishi Temple in Yamagata Prefecture.

Samidare o
Atsumete hayashi
Mogami-gawa

The lasting early summer rains increased the volume of water in Mogami-gawa to look like a furious rapid.

Meigetsu ya
Ike o megurite
Yomo sugara

Wandering around the pond looking at the beauty of the moon, I just noticed it is already late at night.

Mono ieba
Kuchibiru samushi
Aki no kaze

When I speak ill of others or talk big of myself, I have a bitter aftertaste and feel empty. (The direct interpretation is "The autumn wind feels cold in my mouth when I speak.")

Furuike ya
Kawazu tobokomu
Mizuno oto

Suddenly, a frog jumped into an old pond. The sound broke the silence for the instance, and it went back to the silence again.

Aki fukashi
Tonari ha nanio
Suruhito zo

As a fall deepens, I just feel a bit lonely and wonder things like what my neighbors do.

Basho died in October 1694 at the age of 51. His final poem was written four days prior to his death.

Tabi ni yande
Yume wa kareno o
Kakemeguru

While I am ill in bed on a journey, my heart is still trotting about in the wintery fields in my dreams.

Clockwise, from top left: Takkoku no Iwaya; JR Hiraizumi Station; Zen meditation at Moetsu-ji; Dainichi-do in Chuson-ji; Hiraizumi Station Square; Tsukimi-zaka; Mizukake Mikoshi (festival) at Chuson-ji

Light up at Miyazawa Kenji Dowa Mura (July - Octob

花巻

HANAMAKI

Hanamaki: Idyllic Home of Poet Miyazawa Kenji

The Tohoku earthquake and tsunami of March 11, 2011 took nearly 20,000 lives, including the nearly 3,000 still missing. Japan's Tohoku region suffered devastating damage and is on a long, exhausting path to recovery.

Miyazawa Kenji's poem "Unbeaten by Rain" became a symbol of compassion for the victims and the people's hope for Tohoku's recovery. Kenji was an author of children's literature and poet from Hanamaki City, Iwate Prefecture.

"Unbeaten by Rain" was first recited in connection to the disaster by Ken Watanabe, an actor in Japan and Hollywood, who put on the web shortly after the tsunami disaster and encouraged others to do the same. (kizuna311.com/contents/reading14/) The poem was recited in English at the Washington National Cathedral one month after the disaster at its interfaith service "A Prayer for Japan" and touched many people's hearts. In Hong Kong, Jackie Chan, Alan Tam, and nearly 300 stars composed music for this poem and made a music video.

Kenji's humanity and the spirit of mutual support that the Japanese traditionally value resonated through this poem in many people's hearts regardless of nationality.

"Unbeaten by Rain" by Miyazawa Kenji

Unbeaten by rain
Unbeaten by wind
Unbowed by the snow and the summer heat
Strong in body

Free from greed
Without any anger
Always serene

With a handful of brown rice a day
Miso and a small amount of vegetables suffice

Whatever happens
Consider yourself last, always put others first
Understand from your observation and experience
Never lose sight of these things

In the shadows of the pine groves in the fields
Live modestly under a thatched roof

In the East, if there is a sick child
Go there and take care of him
In the West, if there is an exhausted mother
Go there and relieve her of her burden
In the South, if there is a man near death
Go there and comfort him, tell him "Don't be afraid"
In the North, if there is an argument and a legal dispute
Go there and persuade them it's not worth it

In a drought, shed tears
In a cold summer, carry on
Even with a sense of loss

Being called a fool
Being neither praised nor a burden

Such a person I want to be

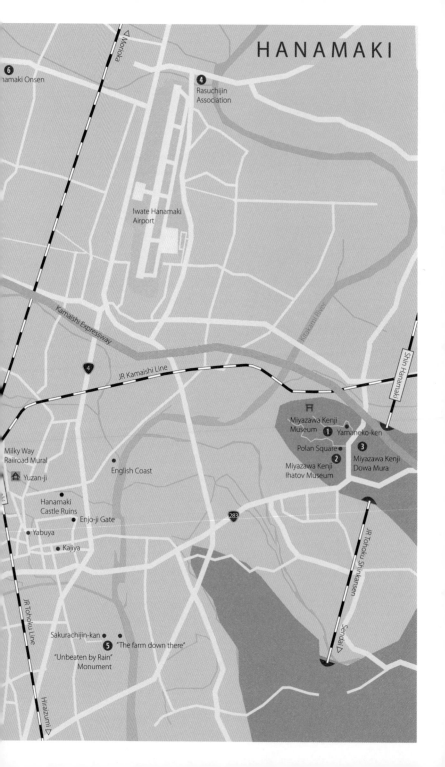

HANAMAKI

6 hamaki Onsen

4 Rasuchijin Association

Iwate Hanamaki Airport

Kamaishi Expressway

Kitakami River

Shin Hanamaki

4 JR Kamaishi Line

Miyazawa Kenji Museum **1**
Yamaneko-ken

Polan Square
2
Miyazawa Kenji Ihatov Museum

3 Miyazawa Kenji Dowa Mura

Milky Way Railroad Mural

Yuzan-ji

English Coast

Hanamaki Castle Ruins
Enjo-ji Gate

Yabuya

Kajiya

283

JR Tohoku Shinkansen

Sendai ▷

Sakurachijin-kan ●
5 ● "The farm down there"

"Unbeaten by Rain" Monument

JR Tohoku Line

Hiraizumi ▷

△ Morioka

Miyazawa Kenji

The enduring, diligent nature Kenji evokes is one of the traits of the people of the Tohoku region. You may remember the quake victims, who patiently endured the hardship with dignity after the disaster, which raised both sympathy and praise from around the world.

Strong earthquakes and tsunamis hit the Tohoku region during the time that Kenji lived. In the year he was born (1896), the Meiji-Sanriku Great Tsunami took over 20,000 lives and another major earthquake, the Rikuu Earthquake, occurred that same year. In the year he died (1933), Tohoku was again hit by a major earthquake and tsunami, the Showa-Sanriku Great Earthquake Tsunami, just six months before he died. One must wonder if it is fate or coincidence that his poem could give courage to the survivors in Tohoku some 80 years later.

While Kenji lived, Tohoku suffered from poor harvests caused by cold weather, and earthquakes and tsunamis further stressed the people's livelihood. There were tragedies where families committed suicide together due to severe poverty; others were forced to sell their daughters for money. Kenji was born in a wealthy family but seeing the poverty of his hometown troubled him a great deal. This and his strong Buddhist faith drove Kenji to struggle to help the poor local farmers in order to improve their standard of living. The enduring spirit of the people of Tohoku moved him and evoked in him a sense of awe.

MIYAZAWA KENJI

"UNBEATEN BY RAIN" WAS FOUND IN A SMALL JOURNAL

The poem "Unbeaten by Rain" was written in 1931, when Kenji was ill. In September, he had gotten a fever during his trip to Tokyo. He at once prepared himself for death and wrote his will, but he managed to recover enough to go back to Hanamaki on November 3, when he wrote this poem in his journal. He did not write it to be read by others, rather as his personal prayer, wishing to have a strong body and mind unbeatable by the rain and wind. He actually wrote the Buddhist chant, "Nam-myoho-renge-kyo," which means "I devote myself to the teachings of the Lotus Sutra," repeatedly at the end of this poem. He passed away two years later in 1933 at the age of 37. The notebook was found inside his favorite suitcase the following year.

MAJOR WORKS OF MIYAZAWA KENJI

In his short life, which lasted only 37 years, Kenji left behind approximately 800 poems and 100 stories, as well as, tanka, haiku, plays and songs. However, only two books—a poetry collection, *Spring and Asura* and a collection of children's stories, *Restaurant of Many Orders*—were published during his lifetime and they did not sell very well at the time. After his death, many more books of his works were published, and today, they even appear in school textbooks. Some of them, including *Milky Way Railroad*, *Matasaburo the Wind Imp*, and *The Restaurant of Many Orders*, have been translated and sold overseas.

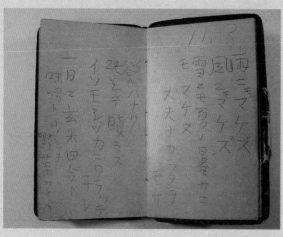

Unbeaton by Rain and Kenji's small journal

Hanamaki City seen from the Miyazawa Kenji Museum

Miyazawa Kenji's roots can be traced in Hanamaki City in Iwate Prefecture, where he was born and grew up. Kenji loved Iwate and created many of his works using this setting. He called this region "Ihatov," a term he coined fondly to sound like Esperanto. He created the image of Ihatov as a dreamland filled with sunlight and breezes of the countryside. In reality, Iwate at this time was a poor farmland region that suffered regularly from famines. He may have wished his homeland to be an ideal paradise, if only in his fantasies.

The nature of the region is utterly magnificent. Although the winters here are very cold and the scenery is covered with deep snow, its mountains are rich in colors, whether it is the green of summer or autumn's reds and oranges. It is filled with abundant sunlight and breezes. In spring, it becomes alive with flowers. The city's name, *Hana*(flower)-*maki*(swirl), is believed to be derived from the beautiful scenery of springtime, when cherry blossom petals fall into the Kitakami River and swirl to create an outstanding sight. Kenji portrayed various images of nature's glory in Iwate. It is actually one of the

MIYAZAWA KENJI

Miyazawa Kenji Museum and Dowa Mura

charms of his stories that you can get a real feeling of magnificent nature.

The first stop on a Miyazawa-inspired trip to Hanamaki should be the Miyazawa Kenji Museum. It is located on a hilltop with a clear view, approximately 1.25 mi (2 km) from the Shin-Hanamaki Station of the Tohoku shinkansen. Traveling from Tokyo, you will realize that the air is so much more refreshing here; you will just want to take a deep breath.

This museum is surrounded with other places of interests related to Kenji, including Miyazawa Kenji Dowa Mura (Miyazawa Kenji's Fantasy Village) where you can experience Kenji's world of children's stories. A flower garden Kenji designed is located at Polan Square, which is named after his work. This neighborhood would be wonderful for a relaxing stroll on a nice day.

The Miyazawa Kenji Museum was built to commemorate the fiftieth anniversary of his death. It displays a wide range of materials, demonstrating Kenji's interest in science, the arts, farming, the environment, and faith, and helping visitors understand the entire universe of his philosophy. He had talent in so many areas that some even call him Japan's Leonardo da Vinci. Along with

Miyazawa Kenji Dowa Mura and Polan Square

other exhibits, you will see his watercolor paintings, his favorite cello and some *ukiyo-e* paintings, which he collected. His handwritten manuscripts show that he revised them repeatedly; he was even known to keep revising his works even after they were thought to be "completed."

Even though this is a small, cozy museum, it holds the most complete collection of artifacts related to Miyazawa Kenji. Many of his belongings and related materials were lost in the air raids in 1945, leaving very few things.

There is a restaurant, Yamaneko-ken (Restaurant Wildcat House)—whose name comes from his famous story "The Restaurant of Many Orders"—next to the museum parking lot.

"The Restaurant of Many Orders" goes: "There was a fine-looking Western-style house. The sign 'Restaurant Wildcat House' was at the door. ... There was a glass door and the sign written in golden letters said 'Please everyone come in. No need to hesitate.'"

The restaurant resembles the description in the story, although there is no wildcat inside who tries to eat his human customers. They serve mainly Japanese dishes

MIYAZAWA KENJI

Yamaneko-ken (Restaurant Wildcat House)

using local ingredients. There is a gift shop inside where Kenji's books and local specialties are sold.

In addition to his writing, Miyazawa was scientist. He entered into the Morioka Agriculture and Forestry College (currently University of Iwate, Agricultural Department), as a top student, and studied geology, agricultural science, and chemistry. He worked as a teacher at the Hanamaki Agricultural High School for four and a half years. In addition to teaching practical agricultural training, he experimented with unique teaching methods, such as singing songs and demonstrating his own plays. His teaching methods are still influential among today's teaching professionals.

After he resigned from teaching, Kenji decided to start farming, living alone. At the age of 30, he established Rasuchijin Association in one of the houses owned by his family, aiming to assist farmers in improving their lives. He gathered young farmers in the area and discussed his ideas on arts for farmers and taught techniques of farming rice and fertilization while working as a farmer himself.

Although Miyazawa Kenji worked hard to realize his dream, having to survive on a coarse diet along with

259

The message board at the Rasuchijin Association building

heavy labor deteriorated his health and is believed to have shortened his life.

Today, the Rasuchijin Association building has been relocated inside the property of the Hanamaki Agricultural High School and is open to public. The building is a simple two-story house, furnished on the first floor with an old organ, a *hibachi*, and round chairs, and it has an atmosphere as if Kenji would just walk in at any moment and start a lecture. There is the message board, "I'm at the farm down there," that still hangs as it was back in those days.

A visitors' notebook at the door features messages written by many visitors from around the country. Some are heartfelt appreciations, for example, a teacher wrote: "I will come back again to see you whenever I'm lost on my way."

You will find a statute of Kenji and his stone memorial, which says: "'What we need is the transparent will holding the galaxy, its huge power and energy.'—Miyazawa Kenji." Even today, the students of the Hanamaki Agricultural High School fondly call the poet Kenji *sensei* (teacher) and pay respect to him in their hearts as a mentor.

MIYAZAWA KENJI

The Kenji Festival

The original location of the Rasuchijin Association building is also a must-see spot for all Kenji fans, even though it is a little bit away from Memorial Museum and other related sites. Three years after Kenji died, a monument of his poem "Unbeaten by Rain" was built here. You may be surprised to see what Kenji called "the farm down there" is not that close by. On his memorial day of September 21, the Kenji Festival is held every year at the field in front of the monument. Kenji fans and scholars gather from around the country and perform recitals of his poems, songs and plays.

Hanamaki City is also known for its hot springs and there are as many as fourteen hot spring towns along the gorge. Kenji visited Osawa Onsen with his students when he was a teacher. At Hanamaki Onsen, one of the largest hot spring resorts in the Tohoku region, there is a solar flower clock that Kenji designed. When Hanamaki Onsen was established in 1923, it was a large-scale resort, including an amusement park, and it has been a very popular place among locals ever since.

Kenji also designed the flower garden on the slope facing the hotel, which was completed in 1927, but has been since changed to a rose garden. You can take a

Osawa Onsen

stroll to the waterfalls of Kamabuchi, which appeared
in Kenji's short story "Dai-gawa" (Dai River), near here.
Many streams of water are falling smoothly down on the
surface of a huge rock, 28 feet high and 100 feet wide.
Kenji brought his students here to study geological
features and rocks around the falls.

As an ecologist and humanist, Kenji's sprit behind
his poem would go beyond the borders and touch
people's hearts everywhere. Away from the center
of Japan's economy, Iwate Prefecture holds humble
treasures that people are rediscovering after the tragedy.
You can experience it when you visit Kenji's ideal
hometown, Ihatov.

Waterfalls of Kamabuchi

MIYAZAWA KENJI

KENJI AND SOBA

In "Unbeaten by Rain", Kenji describes "Eating brown rice and miso and a little vegetables." It is like what is now called a macrobiotic diet. Since Kenji lived as a vegetarian in his last days, after he became a farmer, we tend to believe that he lived all his life on a coarse diet. However, it was not the case in reality. He loved tempura with soba noodles and teriyaki eels over a bowl of rice, visiting a soba restaurant Yabuya in Hanamaki while he was working as a teacher. He had quite an appetite, eating up two orders of tempura soba in one sitting. He could eat fast, too. As he was a language buff, he would call the restaurant "bush," because "yabu" translates to bush in English. He would enjoy eating Western-style food even though it was very rare at the time, especially in Iwate. After all, Kenji was quite a gourmet.

Yabuya, circa 1920

Kenji's favorite menu: tempura with soba noodles and cider

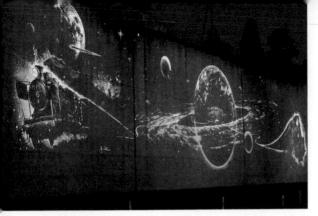

The Milky Way Railroad Mural appears under ultraviolet light at night

Hanamaki City Tourism Information:
Hanamaki Tourism Association
www.kanko-hanamaki.ne.jp/en/

❶ MIYAZAWA KENJI MUSEUM
宮沢賢治記念館

1-1-36 Yazawa, Hanamaki, Iwate
0198-31-2319

This museum displays valuable artifacts related to Kenji, including his favorite belongings and manuscripts, and presents his wide range of interests. Some videos and slides are available.

❷ MIYAZAWA KENJI IHATOV MUSEUM
宮沢賢治イーハトーブ館

1-1-1 Takagi, Hanamaki, Iwate
0198-31-2116

This facility, where Kenji fans and researchers can share information and introduce new research to the public, organizes lectures and workshops about the author.

Miyazawa Kenji Museum

❸ MIYAZAWA KENJI DOWA MURA
宮沢賢治童話村

26-19 Takamatsu, Hanamaki, Iwate
0198-31-2211

This place consists of two parts, Kenji no Gakko (Kenji's School) and Kenji no Kyoshitsu (Kenji's Classroom). Kenji's School is like a theme park where you can share the experience of Kenji's fantasy world. In Kenji's Classroom, you can learn about the plants, animals, planets, birds, and minerals that appear in Kenji's stories. This spacious site, with its pleasant promenade, is an appropriate place for a children's field trip, and a good resource for any adults who are interested in education.

❹ RASUCHIJIN ASSOCIATION
羅須地人協会

Hanamaki Agricultural High School
1-68 Kazura, Hanamaki, Iwate
0198-26-3131

The house where Kenji lived is now relocated inside the Hanamaki Agricultural High School and is maintained by the students. It was formerly one of the houses that the Miyazawa family owned. You can go inside the house, which is kept as it was when Kenji lived alone and taught to local farmers here. There is a statute of Kenji, postured slightly looking down, in the schoolyard.

❺ "UNBEATEN BY RAIN" MONUMENT
「雨ニモマケズ」詩碑

4 Sakura-cho, Hanamaki , Iwate

This monument is located at the original site of Rasuchijin Association, where Kenji lived by himself. The latter half of the poem is inscribed on the monument with the handwriting of Kenji's acquaintance, the famous poet, Takaoka Kotaro. Some of Kenji's ashes and Buddhist scriptures are stored inside the monument. It is located on a hill, overlooking "the farm down there."

The farm down there

Hanamaki hot springs and rose garden

❻ HANAMAKI ONSEN
花巻温泉

Hanamaki Onsen Reservation Center:
0198-37-2111
www.hanamakionsen.co.jp/english

Hanamaki is one of the most popular
hot spring resorts in the Tohoku
region. Because other sightseeing
spots around Hanamaki, like
Hiraizumi and Tohno, have limited
accommodation facilities, Hanamaki
has become the center of tourism
for Iwate Prefecture. The Hotel
Senshukaku's twelve-story building
is actually the tallest building in
Hanamaki-city, where few other
tall buildings exist. On the top floor
of this hotel, there is a popular
restaurant/bar, Prosper. There are two
other hotels next to Senshukaku, and
there is a Japanese-style inn, Keisho-
en, where the imperial family has
stayed. At Keisho-en, unusual for an
inn in hot spring resort, every room
is equipped with a luxurious private

bathtub made of cypress, in addition
to the public baths, and many rooms
have Western-style beds. Each year, over
20,000 visitors from overseas—including
many from Taiwan and Hong Kong—
stay in the this area.

WANKO-SOBA
わんこそば

YABUYA
0198-24-1011
yabuya.jp

KAJIYA
0198-22-3322
kajiya-s.com

One of the popular specialties of
Hanamaki is *wanko-soba*. Instead of
serving an order of soba on a large
plate, they serve it in a tiny bowl and
keep serving you as you eat. The
waitresses swiftly serve the next bowl
of soba into your bowl, which still has
soup inside, right as you finish with
perfect timing. You just have to add the
condiments of your choice, like green
onions and grated horseradish with
nameko mushrooms.

Yabuya

The origin of this dish goes back about 400 years ago. When the lord of the Nambu clan stayed in Hanamaki Castle on his way to Edo, he was served the local specialty soba noodles in an elegant-looking small portion. The Nambu lord loved it and asked for more servings. Eating many servings from a small bowl, the noodles didn't get too soft. The locals started eating it this way after this.

However, another city in Iwate Prefecture, Morioka, also claims that they are the originator of wanko-soba, therefore no one is sure which is the true origin. Both cities hold an eating contest of wanko-soba, where the contestants compete on how many bowls they can finish within the time limit. In Hanamaki, the contest has been held annually on February 11. The record number of bowls is a surprising 254 in just 5 minutes. Wanko-soba eating contests have been held overseas, including in New York (2007) and Berndorf, Austria (2010).

You can enjoy eating wanko-soba casually at popular restaurants, such as Yabuya and Kajiya, where Kenji was once a regular customer. You can eat the freshly boiled handmade soba noodles, mixing them with several condiments to your taste and at your own pace. Although there is no need to challenge eating more or faster in these restaurants, a man from Canada

finished an amazing 200 bowls of soba in October 2011.

You can also enjoy wanko-soba in Hiraizumi. While there are waitresses waiting on the customers to serve more soba in Hanamaki and Morioka, the restaurants in Hiraizumi serve many bowls of soba at the beginning and you can self-serve more soba if you want. For instance, at Basho-kan restaurant in front of Hiraizumi station, one order of wanko-soba will bring 24 bowls of generous servings and will likely leave you feeling full. The self-serving wanko-soba is not as entertaining as the traditional serving style, but it is inexpensive. To prevent the noodles from getting too soft, such restaurants serve the noodles with cold soup, while Hanamaki's version is served hot. There are several wanko-soba restaurants in front of Hiraizumi station and they are easy to find.

HANAMAKI

遠野

T O N O

Oshirasama has been worshipped in homes of old families as the god of silk production, Tono City Museum

Tono: Home of Japanese Folktales

Located one hour from Shin-Hanamaki station on the JR Kamaishi line, Tono is considered a home of Japanese folktales. *Tono Monogatari* is a collection of legendary folktales from around this area, written by Yanagida Kunio, which has been read continuously for the last 100 years. Yanagida is known as the father of Japanese folklore.

HOME OF JAPANESE FOLKTALES

Tono's climate is severe. The people here have to endure deep snow during the winter. They have feared and worshiped nature, and have learned to survive in it with harmony. The folktales were inspired by the lives of such people.

Tono Monogatari collects mysterious folktales that people had passed on through the generations, stories that describe the origins of deities, and creatures such as Tengu, Kappa, and Zashiki-warashi. The roots of Japanese spirits are here.

Among them, the folktales about Kappa are most famous.

What is the Kappa after all? This creature is a kind of specter, or in one theory, a cryptid, like Bigfoot or the Loch Ness Monster.

The Japanese believe in the existence of many different gods, "Yaoyorozu no Kami," literally meaning eight million gods. They believe that there are gods within nature and everything around them. Some believe that the Kappa are a spirit of the water. They are said to live in numerous rivers and streams, and possibly were created as a warning to keep children from drowning.

About the size of a child, the Kappa in Tono have a shell on their back like turtles, a dish on their head, webbed hands and feet, and a sharp beak-like mouth.

Kappa Buchi shrine

Fishing at Kappa Buchi

Kappa Buchi (Kappa Brink) is where it is believed that many Kappa live and scare people by playing tricks on them. Kappa love clear water. They are believed to have water in the dish on their heads and lose their power or die if the dish becomes dry. This brink by the stream is surrounded by dense bushes, creating the feeling that a Kappa might appear in any moment. There is a small shrine by the shore of this stream, which is dedicated to the Kappa deity.

For most Japanese, the image of Kappa is like a likable neighbor, rather than a scary monster. Kappa often appear as a hero in animation or *manga*, or as a character in ads, and are widely popular among the Japanese. The sushi roll with cucumber inside is called *kappa-maki* because it is believed that Kappa like cucumbers.

One cannot help but get swept up in the Kappa excitement. For those who which to encounter the creature, the Tono Tourism Association issues the "Permit for Catching Kappa" (200 yen), which is quite popular. On the back of this permit, there are seven warnings for catching Kappa: (1) You cannot harm

Nambu *magariya* at Tono Furusato Village

HOME OF JAPANESE FOLKTALES

Living room ia the *magariya* at Tono Furusato Village and the Chiba family house

Kappa and have to catch them alive. And so on. You can enjoy such playfulness

Tono maintains more traditional culture than just folktales. Nanbu *magariya* (Southern bent house) is a traditional house with a thatched roof, whose residence quarters and horse stable are connected in an L-shape. These houses look like small hills or mountains blending into the natural landscape. Today, only a few families actually live in these houses. The Chiba family's house is one of those and they let visitors come in to see the inside of the house. You may also find some lodging in these traditional houses.

Along with tradition, in Tono, you can feel the existence of the gods, who are living in many things in nature, close to you. Here is the spirit of Japan, which is very difficult to find in the big cities like Tokyo.

Tono Tourism Information:
Visitors' Guide in English
www.tonojikan.jp/Several_languages/
english/english.html

Dobekko (home-brewed sake) Festival at Furusato Village

❶ CHIBA FAMILY NANBU MAGARIYA
南部曲り家　千葉家

1-14, Ayaori-cho Kami-Ayaori, Tono
0198-62-9529

The Chiba family *magariya* is one of the largest in Tono, built about 200 years ago. It is a typical magariya for an upper-class farmer's house, built at the peak of this building style, with fine features like stone walls and fences surrounding it. The record shows 25 people, including servants, lived in the house with 20 horses. It is a nationally designated cultural property.

❷ TONO FURUSATO VILLAGE
遠野ふるさと村

5-89-1, Tsukimoushi-cho Kami-Tsukimoushi, Tono
0198-64-2300
www.tono-furusato.jp/index.html

A traditional local village is recreated here, where you can experience the lifestyle of a mountain village and learn its culture. There is a *magariya* with a thatched roof, rice paddies, farmland, charcoal burning lodge, and waterwheels. Some local elders are farming here as *maburitto* (keepers). They can show you how to make crafts with straw and bamboo. You can try out *mochi-tsuki*, pounding rice cakes, and hand-making soba noodles. If you understand Japanese, try to listen to *kataribe* (storytellers) telling old stories.

The Chiba family *magariya*

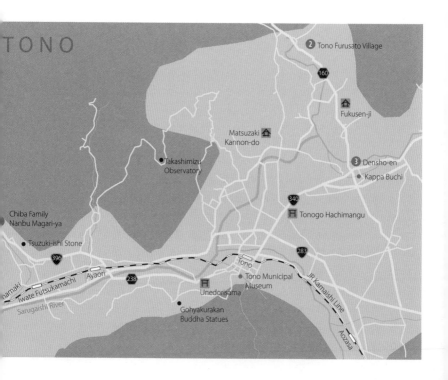

TONO

❷ Tono Furusato Village

160

⛩ Fukusen-ji

Matsuzaki ⛩
Kannon-do

● Takashimizu
Observatory

❸ Densho-en

● Kappa Buchi

340

⛩ Tonogo Hachimangu

Chiba Family
Nanbu Magari-ya

● Tsuzuki-ishi Stone

396

Tono

283

Ayaori

238

Iwate Futsukamachi

● Tono Municipal
Museum

JR Kamaishi Line

⛩ Unedorisama

Sarugaishi River

Aozasa

● Gohyakurakan
Buddha Statues

❸ DENSHOEN
伝承園

6-5-1, Tsuchibuchi-cho Tsuchibuchi,
Tono
0198-62-8655
www.densyoen.jp/index.html

Experience a traditional farmer's lifestyle
at this living museum. You can make
local crafts and listen to the folktales.
There is the *magariya* house of the
Kikuchi family, which is designated as a
nationally important cultural property,
and a restaurant serving local dishes.

Oshira-sama (god of silk production) dolls at Denshoen

273

TONO SCENES

Clockwise, from top left: Tono Valley; JR Kamaishi Line; Gohyakurakan Buddha statues; Aragami Shrine; a winter scene of Tono Frusato Village; Tsuzuki-ishi Stone; a horse at a traditional *magariya*

Miracle Pine Tree
at Rikuzentakata

It's been years since the deadly earthquake and tsunami ravaged Tohoku in 2011. An 88-foot pine tree refused to succumb to the onslaught. It stood as the last remaining member of what was once a forest of 70,000 trees along the coast in Rikuzentakata, Iwate prefecture. Now a massive sculpture stands to memorialize that special tree, and serves as a quiet reminder of nature's power.

INDEX

CREDITS

ACKNOWLEDGEMENTS

Museyon would like to thank the many people and institutions who helped in the creation of this book

Azuchi Castle Museum
Azuchi-cho, Omihachiman
0748-46-5616
www.azuchi-shiga.com/n-jyoukakusiry-oukan.htm

Chuson-ji Temple
Hiraizumi, Iwate
0191-46-2211
www.chusonji.or.jp/en/

Daitoku-ji Temple, Soken-in
Kita-ku, Kyoto
075-492-2630

Edo-Tokyo Museum
Sumida-ku, Tokyo
03-3626-9974
www.edo-tokyo-museum.or.jp/en/

Ghibli Museum, Mitaka
Mitaka, Tokyo
0570-055777
www.ghibli-museum.jp/en/welcome/

Hanamaki Tourism Association
Hanamaki, Iwate
0198-29-4522
www.kanko-hanamaki.ne.jp/en/

Hiraizumi Tourism Association
Hiraizumi-cho, Iwate
0191-46-2110
hiraizumi.or.jp/en/index.html

Icom Co., Ltd. / Kyoto Syunju
Nakagyo-ku, Kyoto
075-231-6415
icom-kyotosyunjyu.com/english-top/

Iwate Prefectural Government Department of Commerce, Industry, Lador and Tourism
Morioka, Iwate
019-629-5574
www.japan-iwate.info/index.html

Japan National Tourism Organization
(JNTO)
New York Office
New York, NY
212-757-5640

www.jnto.go.jp/eng/

Tokyo Office
Chiyoda-ku, Tokyo
03-3201-3331

Kobe City Museum
Chuo-ku, Kobe, Hyogo
078-391-0035
www.city.kobe.lg.jp/museum/

Kyoto Convention & Visitors Bureau
Nakagyo-Ku, Kyoto
75-212-4140
meetkyoto.jp/en/

Miyagi Prefecture Government Tourism Division
Sendai, Miyagi
022-211-2822
www.pref.miyagi.jp/site/kankou-en/

Nobunaga no Yakata
(Hose of Nobunaga)
Azuchi-cho, Omihachiman
0748-46-6512
www.zc.ztv.ne.jp/bungei/nobu/

Pokémon Center Tokyo
Minato-ku, Tokyo
03-6430-7733
www.pokemon.co.jp/gp/pokecen/english/

The Sakamoto Ryoma Memorial Museum
Kochi City, Kochi
088-841-0001
www.ryoma-kinenkan.jp/en/

The Tale of Genji Museum
Uji, Kyoto
774-39-9300
www.uji-genji.jp/en/

Teradaya
Fushimi, Kyoto
075-622-0243

Tokugawa Art Museum
Higashi-ku, Nagoya, Aich
052-935-6261
www.tokugawa-art-museum.jp/

Tokyo National Museum
Taito-ku, Tokyo

03-5405-8686
www.tnm.jp

Tono City Museum
Tono, Iwate
0198-62-2340
www.city.tono.iwate.jp/index.cfm/25,10265,122,144,html

Tono Tourism Association
Tono, Iwate
0198-62-1333
http://www.tonojikan.jp/Several_languages/english/english.html

Uji City Chamber of Commerce and Tourism Bureau
Uji, Kyoto
0774-22-3141
http://www.city.uji.kyoto.jp/en/

Uji City Tourist Association
Uji, Kyoto
0774-23-3334
http://www.kyoto-uji-kankou.or.jp/index-en.html

Yabuya
Hanamaki, Iwate
0198-24-1011
yabuya.jp

Yonezawa City Uesugi Museum
Yonezawa, Yamagata
0238-26-8001
www.denkoku-no-mori.yonezawa.yamagata.jp/uesugi.htm

ABOUT MUSEYON

Named after the Museion, the ancient Egyptian institute dedicated to the muses, Museyon Guides is an independent publisher that explores the world through the lens of cultural obsessions. Intended for frequent fliers and armchair travelers alike, our books are expert-curated and carefully researched, offering rich visuals, practical tips and quality information.

MUSEYON'S OTHER TITLES

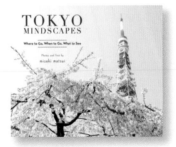

Cool Japan Series, Book 2
TOKYO MINDSCAPES
Where to Go, When to Go, What to See
By misaki matsui
ISBN 9781940842325

Pick one up and follow your interests…wherever they might go.
For more information vist **www.museyon.com**, **facebook.com/museyon**, **twitter.com/museyon or instagram.com/museyonbooks**

Publisher: Akira Chiba
Editor: Heather Corcoran, Janice Battiste
Translators: Mariko Shii Gharbi, Claire Samuels

Cover Design: José Antonio Contreras
Photographer: Misaki Matsui

Museyon Guides has made every effort to verify that all information included in this guide is accurate and current as of our press date. All details are subject to change.

ABOUT THE AUTHOR

Sumiko Kajiyama is a journalist and scriptwriter residing in Japan. After working as a TV show director at KTV in Osaka, she lived in the U.S. for more than eight years while getting her Master of Media Communication from New York University and working at *The Yomiuri America* newspaper. Her books include *GHIBLI Magic*, *The Man Who Changed Animation Business*, *The Creative Work Style by Top Producers*, and *New Rules to Be Happy with Your Work*.